MELODY • LYRICS • CHORDS

W9-CZM-616

FOR ALL "C" INSTRUMENTS

THE MOVIE FAKE BOOK

5th EDITION

INCLUDES OVER 500 SONGS & THEMES

ISBN 978-0-7935-8244-0

HAL•LEONARD®
CORPORATION

7777 W. BLUEMOUND RD. P.O. BOX 13819 MILWAUKEE, WI 53213

Visit Hal Leonard Online at
www.halleonard.com

SONG LISTING

* Means that the song existed before the movie was made and was featured in the film cited. Otherwise, the song was written directly for the screen.

MOVIE LISTING

CHRONOLOGICAL LISTING

Year	Movie	Song Title	Page

'50s

16

'80s

AC-CENT-TCHU-ATE THE POSITIVE
from the Motion Picture HERE COME THE WAVES

Lyric by JOHNNY MERCER
Music by HAROLD ARLEN

THE ADDAMS FAMILY THEME
Theme from the TV Show and Movie

Music and Lyrics by
VIC MIZZY

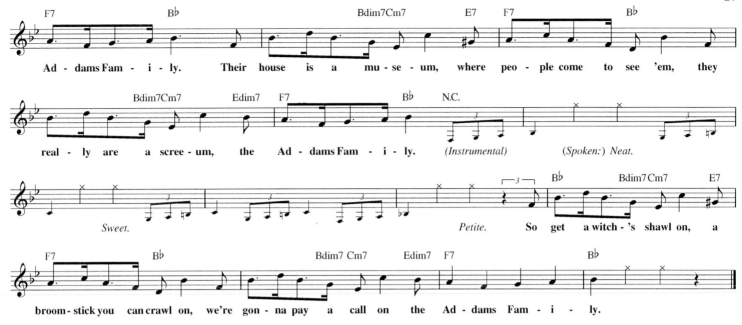

Ad - dams Fam - i - ly. Their house is a mu - se - um, where peo - ple come to see 'em, they

real - ly are a scree - um, the Ad - dams Fam - i - ly. *(Instrumental)* *(Spoken:)* Neat.

Sweet. *Petite.* So get a witch - 's shawl on, a

broom - stick you can crawl on, we're gon - na pay a call on the Ad - dams Fam - i - ly.

AIN'T MISBEHAVIN'
from AIN'T MISBEHAVIN'

Words by ANDY RAZAF
Music by THOMAS "FATS" WALLER and HARRY BROOKS

Medium Swing

No one to talk with, all by my - self, no one to walk with, but I'm hap - py on ___ the shelf,

Ain't mis - be - hav - in' I'm sav - in' my love for you. ___ I know for cer - tain

the one I love, I'm thru with flirt - in' it's just you I'm think - in' of. Ain't mis - be - hav - in'

I'm sav - in' my love for you. ___ Like Jack Horn - er in the cor - ner

don't go no - where, what do I care, Your kiss - es are worth wait - in' for, be -

lieve me. I don't stay out late, don't care to go. I'm home a - bout eight, just

me and my ra - di - o, Ain't mis - be - hav - in' I'm sav - in' my love for you. ___

AGAINST ALL ODDS
(Take a Look at Me Now)
from AGAINST ALL ODDS

Words and Music by
PHIL COLLINS

AIN'T THERE ANYONE HERE FOR LOVE
from the Motion Picture GENTLEMEN PREFER BLONDES

Lyric by HAROLD ADAMSON
Music by HOAGY CARMICHAEL

AIN'T TOO PROUD TO BEG
featured in THE BIG CHILL

Words and Music by EDWARD HOLLAND
and NORMAN WHITFIELD

Additional Lyrics

2. Now I've heard a cryin' man
   Is half a man with no sense of pride,
   But if I have to cry to keep you,
   I don't mind weepin' if it'll keep you by my side.
   Chorus

3. If I have to sleep on your doorstep all night and day
   Just to keep you from walking away,
   Let your friends laugh, even this I can stand,
   'Cause I wanna keep you any way I can.
   Chorus

4. Now I've got a love so deep in the pit of my heart,
   And each day it grows more and more,
   I'm not ashamed to call and plead to you, baby,
   If pleading keeps you from walking out that door.
   Chorus

AIRPORT LOVE THEME
(Winds of Chance)
from AIRPORT

Words by PAUL FRANCIS WEBSTER
Music by ALFRED NEWMAN

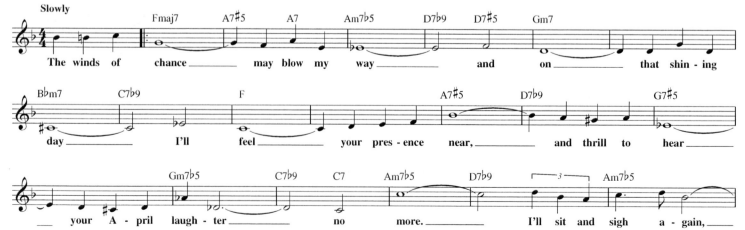

ALFIE
Theme from the Paramount Picture ALFIE

Words by HAL DAVID
Music by BURT BACHARACH

26

ALICE IN WONDERLAND
from Walt Disney's ALICE IN WONDERLAND

© 1951 Walt Disney Music Company
Copyright Renewed

Words by BOB HILLIARD
Music by SAMMY FAIN

ALL FOR LOVE
from Walt Disney Pictures' THE THREE MUSKETEERS

Words and Music by BRYAN ADAMS,
R. J. LANGE and MICHAEL KAMEN

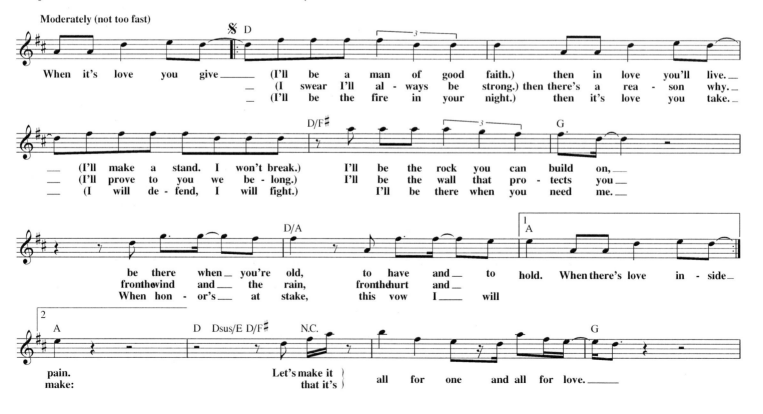

ALL OF MY LIFE
from THE MIRROR HAS TWO FACES

Music by BARBRA STREISAND and MARVIN HAMLISCH
Lyrics by ALAN and MARILYN BERGMAN

ALL OF YOU
from SILK STOCKINGS

Words and Music by
COLE PORTER

ALL THE WAY
from THE JOKER IS WILD

Words by SAMMY CAHN
Music by JAMES VAN HEUSEN

ALMOST PARADISE
Love Theme from the Paramount Motion Picture FOOTLOOSE

Words by DEAN PITCHFORD
Music by ERIC CARMEN

ALSO SPRACH ZARATHUSTRA
featured in the Motion Picture 2001: A SPACE ODYSSEY

By RICHARD STRAUSS

AMARCORD
Theme from the Film AMARCORD

By NINO ROTA

AMERICA
from the Motion Picture THE JAZZ SINGER

Words and Music by
NEIL DIAMOND

AN AMERICAN SYMPHONY
from MR. HOLLAND'S OPUS

Composed by
MICHAEL KAMEN

ANIMAL CRACKERS IN MY SOUP
from CURLY TOP

Lyrics by TED KOEHLER and IRVING CAESAR
Music by RAY HENDERSON

AND ALL THAT JAZZ
from CHICAGO

Words by FRED EBB
Music by JOHN KANDER

ANIMAL HOUSE
Theme from the Universal Picture ANIMAL HOUSE

Words and Music by
STEPHEN BISHOP

ANOTHER SUITCASE IN ANOTHER HALL
from EVITA

Words by TIM RICE
Music by ANDREW LLOYD WEBBER

ANYTHING YOU CAN DO
from the Stage Production ANNIE GET YOUR GUN

Words and Music by
IRVING BERLIN

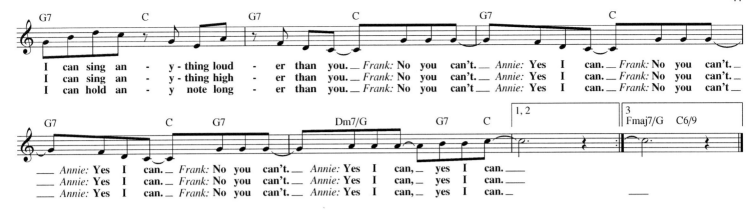

I can sing an‑y‑thing loud‑er than you. *Frank:* No you can't. *Annie:* Yes I can. *Frank:* No you can't.
I can sing an‑y‑thing high‑er than you. *Frank:* No you can't. *Annie:* Yes I can. *Frank:* No you can't.
I can hold an‑y note long‑er than you. *Frank:* No you can't *Annie:* Yes I can. *Frank:* No you can't

___ *Annie:* Yes I can. ___ *Frank:* No you can't. ___ *Annie:* Yes I can, ___ yes I can. ___
___ *Annie:* Yes I can. ___ *Frank:* No you can't. ___ *Annie:* Yes I can, ___ yes I can. ___
___ *Annie:* Yes I can. ___ *Frank:* No you can't. ___ *Annie:* Yes I can, ___ yes I can. ___

ANYWHERE I WANDER
from the Motion Picture HANS CHRISTIAN ANDERSEN

By FRANK LOESSER

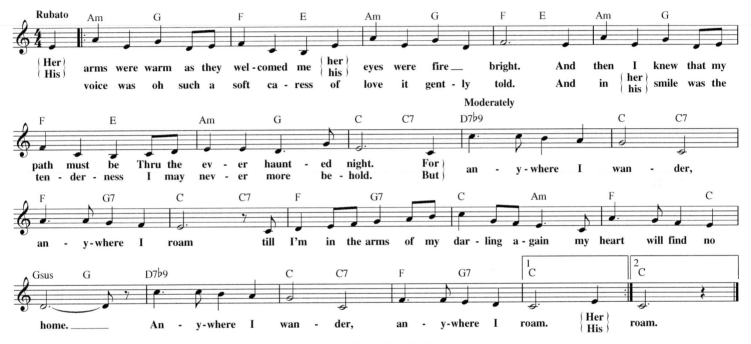

{Her / His} arms were warm as they wel‑comed me {her / his} eyes were fire ___ bright. And then I knew that my
voice was oh such a soft ca‑ress of love it gent‑ly told. And in {her / his} smile was the

path must be Thru the ev‑er haunt‑ed night. For
ten‑der‑ness I may nev‑er more be‑hold. But } an‑y‑where I wan‑der,

an‑y‑where I roam till I'm in the arms of my dar‑ling a‑gain my heart will find no

home. ___ An‑y‑where I wan‑der, an‑y‑where I roam. {Her / His} roam.

AROUND THE WORLD
from AROUND THE WORLD IN EIGHTY DAYS

Words and Music by VICTOR YOUNG
and HAROLD ADAMSON

A‑round the world I've searched for you, I trav‑eled on when hope was

gone to keep a ren‑dez‑vous. I knew some‑where, some‑time, some‑how, you'd look at

me and I would see the smile you're smil‑ing now. It might have been in Count‑y

Down, or in New York, in Gay Pa‑ree, or e‑ven Lon‑don Town. No more will

I go all a‑round the world, for I have found my world in you.

ARRIVEDERCI ROMA
(Goodbye To Rome)
from the Motion Picture SEVEN HILLS OF ROME

Words and Music by CARL SIGMAN, RANUCCI RENATO,
SANDRO GIOVANNI and PEIDRO GARINEI

AXEL F
Theme from the Paramount Motion Picture BEVERLY HILLS COP

By HAROLD FALTERMEYER

BABY ELEPHANT WALK
from the Paramount Picture HATARI!

Words by HAL DAVID
Music by HENRY MANCINI

BABY, IT'S COLD OUTSIDE
from the Motion Picture NEPTUNE'S DAUGHTER

By FRANK LOESSER

Moderately

F   Fmaj7   F6   Fmaj7   Gm7   C7

I real - ly can't stay _____ I've got to go 'way. _____
sim - ply must go _____ the ans - wer is No!

But ba - by, it's cold _ out - side! _ But ba - by, it's cold _
But ba - by, it's cold out - side! _ But ba - by, it's cold _

Gm7   C7   F   Fmaj7   F6   F   F9

This eve - ning has been _____ so ver - y nice. _____
The wel - come has been _____ so nice and warm.

_ out - side! _ Been hop - ing that you'd _ drop in! _ I'll hold your hands _
_ out - side! _ How luck - y that you _ dropped in! _ Look out the win -

Bb6   Bb9

My moth - er will start to wor - ry _____ and fa - ther will be pac - ing the
My sis - ter will be sus - pi - cious _____ my broth - er will be there at the

_ they're just like ice. Beau - ti - ful, what's your hur - ry? _
_ dow at that storm. Gosh, your lips look de - li - cious. _

F6   G7

floor. So real - ly I'd bet - ter scur - ry, _____ well, may - be just a half a drink
door. My maid - en aunt's mind is vi - cious _ well, may - be just a ci - ga - rette

Lis - ten to the fi - re - place roar! Beau - ti - ful, please, don't hur - ry. _
waves up - on a trop - ic - al shore! Gosh, your lips are de - li - cious _

C7   F   Fmaj7   F6   Fmaj7

more. The neigh - bors might think _____ say,
more. I've got to get home _____ say,

Put some re - cords on while I pour. _ But, ba - by, it's bad _ out there; _
nev - er such a bliz - zard be - fore. _ But, ba - by, you'd freeze _ out there; _

Gm7   C7   Gm7   C7   F   Fmaj7   F6   F

what's in this drink? _____ I wish I knew how _____ to break the
lend me a comb. You've real - ly been grand _____ but don't you

no cabs to be had _ out there. _ Your eyes are like star - light now _
it's up to your knees _ out there. _ I thrill when you touch _ my hand _

BACK IN THE SADDLE AGAIN

Words and Music by GENE AUTRY
and RAY WHITLEY

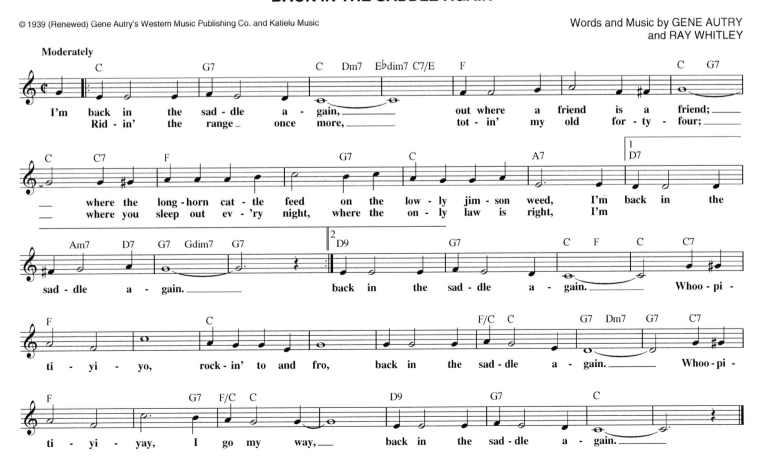

BACK TO THE FUTURE
from the Universal Motion Picture BACK TO THE FUTURE

By ALAN SILVESTRI

THE BALLAD OF DAVY CROCKETT
from Walt Disney's DAVY CROCKETT

Words by TOM BLACKBURN
Music by GEORGE BRUNS

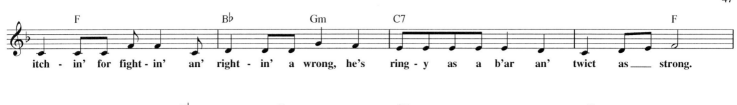

BALLAD OF EASY RIDER
from EASY RIDER

Words and Music by
ROGER McGUINN

BALLAD OF CAT BALLOU

Words by MACK DAVID
Music by JERRY LIVINGSTON

THE BARE NECESSITIES
from Walt Disney's THE JUNGLE BOOK

Words and Music by
TERRY GILKYSON

BE CAREFUL, IT'S MY HEART
from HOLIDAY INN

Words and Music by
IRVING BERLIN

BE OUR GUEST
from Walt Disney's BEAUTY AND THE BEAST

Lyrics by HOWARD ASHMAN
Music by ALAN MENKEN

BEAUTIFUL BOY
(Darling Boy)
from MR. HOLLAND'S OPUS

Words and Music by
JOHN LENNON

BEAUTY AND THE BEAST
from Walt Disney's BEAUTY AND THE BEAST

Lyrics by HOWARD ASHMAN
Music by ALAN MENKEN

BELIEVE
from Warner Bros. Pictures' THE POLAR EXPRESS

Words and Music by GLEN BALLARD
and ALAN SILVESTRI

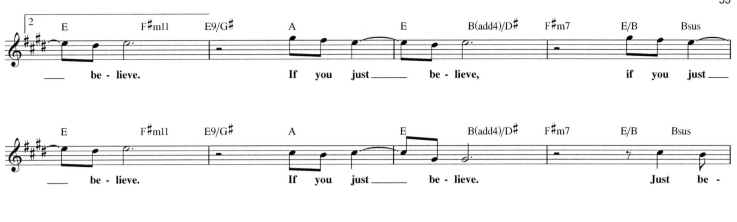

BE A CLOWN
from THE PIRATE

Words and Music by
COLE PORTER

BELLA NOTTE
(This Is the Night)
from Walt Disney's LADY AND THE TRAMP

Words and Music by PEGGY LEE
and SONNY BURKE

BEN

Words by DON BLACK
Music by WALTER SCHARF

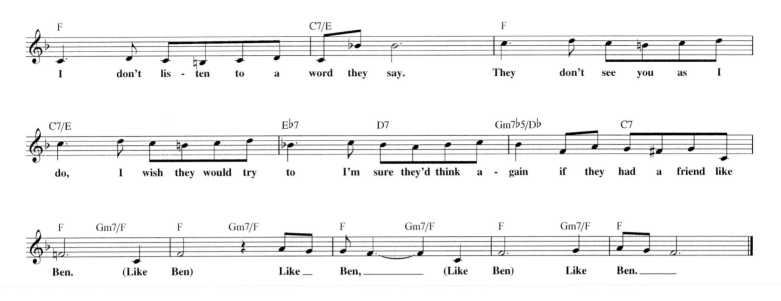

THE BEST THINGS HAPPEN WHILE YOU'RE DANCING
from the Motion Picture Irving Berlin's WHITE CHRISTMAS

Words and Music by
IRVING BERLIN

BETTY BOOP
from the Paramount Cartoon

Words by EDWARD HEYMAN
Music by JOHN W. GREEN

BEYOND THE BLUE HORIZON
from the Paramount Picture MONTE CARLO

Words by LEO ROBIN
Music by RICHARD A. WHITING and W. FRANKE HARLING

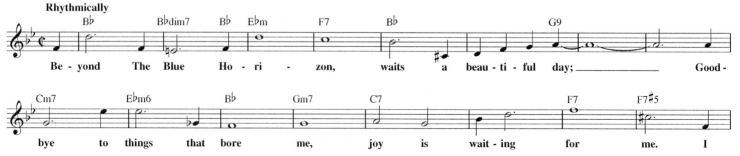

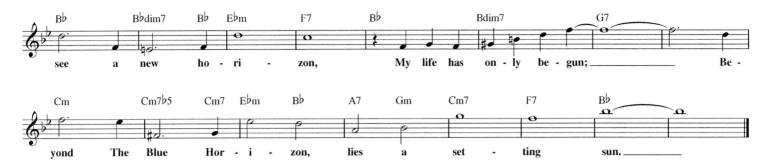

BEYOND THE SEA
featured in the Walt Disney/Pixar film FINDING NEMO

By ALBERT LASRY and
CHARLES TRENET
English Lyrics by JACK LAWRENCE

BIBBIDI-BOBBIDI-BOO
(The Magic Song)
from Walt Disney's CINDERELLA

Words by JERRY LIVINGSTON
Music by MACK DAVID and AL HOFFMAN

Brightly

Sa - la - ga - doo - la men - chic - ka boo - la bib - bi - di - bob - bi - di - boo, put 'em to - geth - er and what have you got

bib - bi - di - bob - bi - di - boo. Sa - la - ga - doo - la men - chic - ka boo - la bib - bi - di - bob - bi - di - boo,

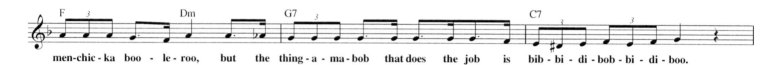

it - 'll do mag - ic be - lieve it or not, bib - bi - di - bob - bi - di - boo. Sa - la - ga - doo - la means

men - chic - ka boo - le - roo, but the thing - a - ma - bob that does the job is bib - bi - di - bob - bi - di - boo.

Sa - la - ga - doo - la men - chic - ka boo - la bib - bi - di - bob - bi - di - boo, put 'em to - geth - er and what have you got

bib - bi - di - bob - bi - di bib - bi - di - bob - bi - di bib - bi - di - bob - bi - di - boo.

BIG SPENDER
from SWEET CHARITY

Music by CY COLEMAN
Lyrics by DOROTHY FIELDS

Moderately, with a beat

The min - ute you walked in the joint, I could see you were a man of dis - tinc - tion, a

real big spend - er, good look - ing, so re - fined. _ Say, would - n't you like to know what's go - ing

on in my mind? _ So let me get right to the point, I don't pop my cork for ev - 'ry guy I see. _

To Coda

_ Hey! Big spend - er, spend a lit - tle time _ with me.

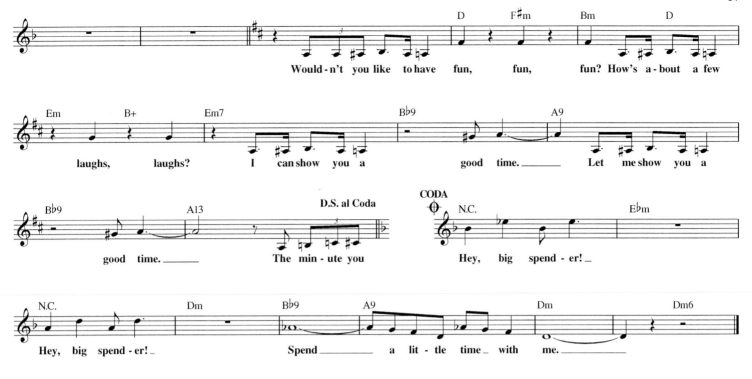

BLUE HAWAII
from the Paramount Picture WAIKIKI WEDDING
Theme from the Paramount Picture BLUE HAWAII

Words and Music by LEO ROBIN
and RALPH RAINGER

BLAME CANADA
from the Motion Picture Soundtrack SOUTH PARK: BIGGER, LONGER & UNCUT

Words and Music by TREY PARKER
and MARC SHAIMAN

BLAZE OF GLORY
featured in the film YOUNG GUNS II

Words and Music by
JON BON JOVI

BLESS THE BEASTS AND CHILDREN
from BLESS THE BEASTS AND CHILDREN

Words and Music by BARRY DeVORZON
and PERRY BOTKIN, JR.

BLUE VELVET
featured in the Motion Picture BLUE VELVET

Words and Music by BERNIE WAYNE
and LEE MORRIS

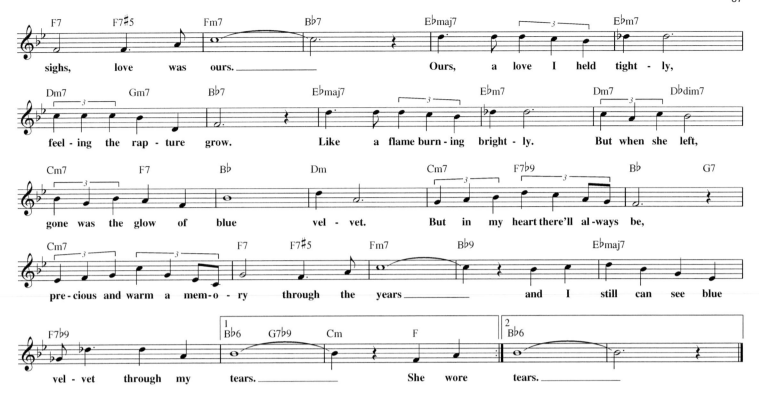

sighs, love was ours._____ Ours, a love I held tight-ly, feel-ing the rap-ture grow. Like a flame burn-ing bright-ly. But when she left, gone was the glow of blue vel-vet. But in my heart there'll al-ways be, pre-cious and warm a mem-o-ry through the years_____ and I still can see blue vel-vet through my tears._____ She wore tears._____

BOOGIE WOOGIE BUGLE BOY
from BUCK PRIVATES

Words and Music by DON RAYE
and HUGHIE PRINCE

They made him blow a bu-gle for his Un-cle Sam,__ it real-ly brought him down be-cause he
puts the boys to sleep with "boo-gie" ev-'ry night,__ and wakes them up the same way in the

could-n't jam.__ The cap-tain seemed to un-der-stand__ be-cause the
ear-ly bright.__ They clap their hands and stamp their feet__ be-cause they

next day the "cap" went out and draft-ed a band,__ and now the com-p'ny jumps
know how he plays__ when some-one gives him a beat,__ he real-ly breaks it up } when he plays

re-veil-le, he's the boo-gie woo-gie bu-gle boy of Com-pa-ny B.__ A toot! A toot! A

toot did dle ah-da toot. He blows it eight to the bar__ in "boo-gie" rhy-thm. He can't blow a note un-less a

bass and gui-tar__ is play-in' with 'im. He makes the com-p'ny jump when he plays

re-veil-le, he's the boo-gie woo-gie bu-gle boy of Com-pa-ny B!__ He Com-pa-ny B!__

BOHEMIAN RHAPSODY

featured in the Motion Picture WAYNE'S WORLD
from HIGH SCHOOL HIGH

Words and Music by
FREDDIE MERCURY

A BOAT ON THE SEA
from GRACE OF MY HEART

Words and Music by LARRY KLEIN
and DAVID BAERWALD

BORN FREE

from the Columbia Pictures' Release BORN FREE

Words by DON BLACK
Music by JOHN BARRY

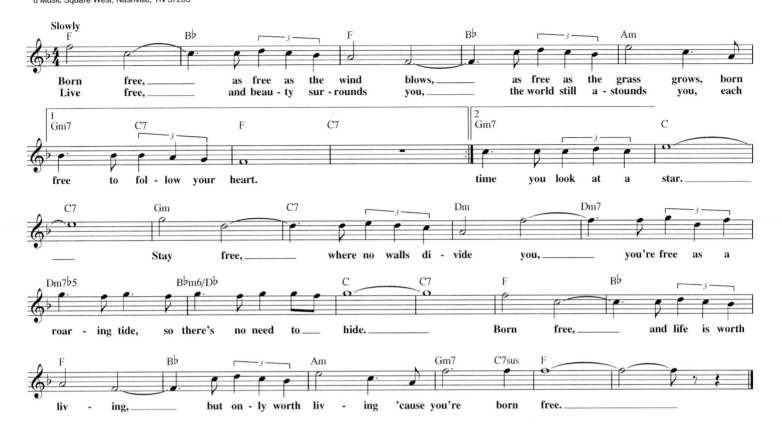

Born free,_____ as free as the wind blows,_____ as free as the grass grows, born
Live free,_____ and beau - ty sur - rounds you,_____ the world still a - stounds you, each

free to fol - low your heart.

time you look at a star._____

Stay free,_____ where no walls di - vide you,_____ you're free as a

roar - ing tide, so there's no need to ___ hide._____ Born free,_____ and life is worth

liv - ing,_____ but on - ly worth liv - ing 'cause you're born free._____

BORN ON THE FOURTH OF JULY

from BORN ON THE FOURTH OF JULY

Music by
JOHN WILLIAMS

BORN TO BE WILD
from EASY RIDER

Words and Music by
MARS BONFIRE

Moderate Rock beat

Get your mo - tor run - ning. ____ Head out on the high - way ____
I like smoke and light - ning. ____ Heav - y me - tal thun - der ____

look - ing for ad - ven - ture in what - ev - er comes our way. ____
rac - ing in the wind and the feel - ing that I'm un - der. ____

Yeah, dar - ling, gon - na make it hap - pen, take the world in a love em - brace. ____

Fire ____ all of your guns ____ at once ____ and ex - plode _ in - to space. ____

Like a true ____ na - ture child ____ we were born, ____ born to be wild. ____

We have climbed ____ so high, ____ nev - er want to die. ____

Born to be wild, ____ born to be wild. ____

D.C. (Lyric 1)   Repeat and Fade

Born to be wild. ____

THE BOYS IN THE BACKROOM

Words and Music by FRANK LOESSER
and FREDERICK HOLLANDER

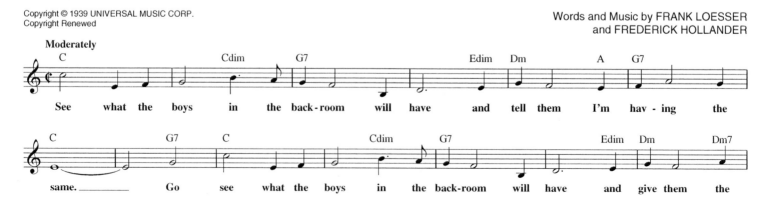

Moderately

See what the boys in the back - room will have and tell them I'm hav - ing the

same. ____ Go see what the boys in the back - room will have and give them the

BREAKFAST AT TIFFANY'S
Theme from the Paramount Picture BREAKFAST AT TIFFANY'S

Music by HENRY MANCINI

BREAKAWAY
from THE PRINCESS DIARIES 2: ROYAL ENGAGEMENT

Words and Music by BRIDGET BENENATE,
AVRIL LAVIGNE and MATTHEW GERRARD

BREAKING FREE
from the Disney Channel Original Movie HIGH SCHOOL MUSICAL

Words and Music by
JAMIE HOUSTON

(THE BOYS ARE) BACK IN TOWN
from the Paramount Motion Picture 48 HRS

Words and Music by
BRIAN O'NEAL

Additional Lyrics

2. I know that ev'rybody when they hear the music will be doin' it on the floor.
   Jump up and down then turn around and tell the band to play, play some more.
   So, tonight you can dance and romance and do anything you feel like doin';
   So, don't look surprised 'cause you know what I like, and tonight we ought to do it.
   Chorus

BUTTONS AND BOWS
from the Paramount Picture THE PALEFACE

Words and Music by JAY LIVINGSTON
and RAY EVANS

Lively

East is east and west is west and the wrong one I have chose; Let's go where you'll
bur - y me in this prai - rie, take me where the ce - ment grows; Let's move down to

keep on wear - in' those frills and flow - ers and But-tons And Bows. Rings and things and But-tons And Bows.
some big town where they love a gal by the cut of her clothes, and you'll stand out in But-tons And Bows.

CA, C'EST L'AMOUR
from LES GIRLS

Words and Music by
COLE PORTER

CABARET
from the Musical CABARET

Words by FRED EBB
Music by JOHN KANDER

CALL ME
from the Paramount Motion Picture AMERICAN GIGOLO

Words by DEBORAH HARRY
Music by GIORGIO MORODER

CALL ME IRRESPONSIBLE
from the Paramount Picture PAPA'S DELICATE CONDITION

Words by SAMMY CAHN
Music by JAMES VAN HEUSEN

CAN'T HELP FALLING IN LOVE
from the Paramount Picture BLUE HAWAII
from SLIVER

Words and Music by GEORGE DAVID WEISS,
HUGO PERETTI and LUIGI CREATORE

CAN YOU FEEL THE LOVE TONIGHT
from Walt Disney Pictures' THE LION KING

Music by ELTON JOHN
Lyrics by TIM RICE

Freely

Timon: I can see what's hap-p'ning. And they don't have a clue. **Pumbaa: What?** They'll fall in love and here's the bot-tom line: **Who?** Our

tri-o's down to two. **Oh.** The sweet ca-ress of twi-light; there's mag-ic ev-'ry-where. And with all this ro-

Moderately slow
man-tic at-mos-phere,__ dis-as-ter's in the air.

Chorus:
Can you feel __ the love __ to-night,__ the peace the eve-ning brings? The

world, for once,__ in per-fect har-mo-ny __ with all its liv-ing things. **Simba:** So

man-y things__ to tell__ her, but how to make__ her see the truth a-bout__ my past? Im-pos-si-ble.

She'd turn a-way from me. **Nala:** He's hold-ing back,__ he's hid-ing. But what? I can't __ de-cide.__ Why

won't he be__ the king__ I know he is, the king I see in-side? **Chorus: Can** you feel__ the love_

__ to-night,__ the peace the eve-ning brings? The world, for once,__ in

per-fect har-mo-ny __ with all it's liv-ing things.__ Can you feel__ the love_

__ to-night? __ You need-n't look too far. Steal-ing through the night's un-cer-tain-ties,

CANDLE ON THE WATER
from Walt Disney's PETE'S DRAGON

Words and Music by AL KASHA
and JOEL HIRSCHHORN

THE CANDY MAN
from WILLY WONKA AND THE CHOCOLATE FACTORY

Words and Music by LESLIE BRICUSSE
and ANTHONY NEWLEY

THEME FROM "CASINO ROYALE"
from CASINO ROYALE

Words by HAL DAVID
Music by BURT BACHARACH

run with guns ___ and knives, ___ We're fight-ing for our lives.

Have no fear, Bond is here. He's gon-na save the world. Bond is here, have no fear!

CAVATINA
from the Universal Pictures and EMI Films Presentation THE DEER HUNTER

By STANLEY MYERS

Slowly, with feeling

CHANGE PARTNERS
from the RKO Radio Motion Picture CAREFREE

Words and Music by
IRVING BERLIN

CHANGE THE WORLD
featured on the Motion Picture Soundtrack PHENOMENON

Words and Music by WAYNE KIRKPATRICK,
GORDON KENNEDY and TOMMY SIMS

CHARIOTS OF FIRE

Music by VANGELIS

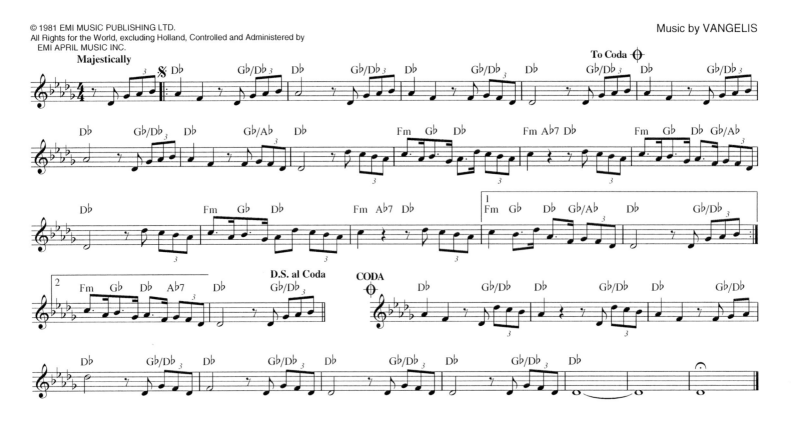

CHEEK TO CHEEK
from the RKO Radio Motion Picture TOP HAT

Words and Music by
IRVING BERLIN

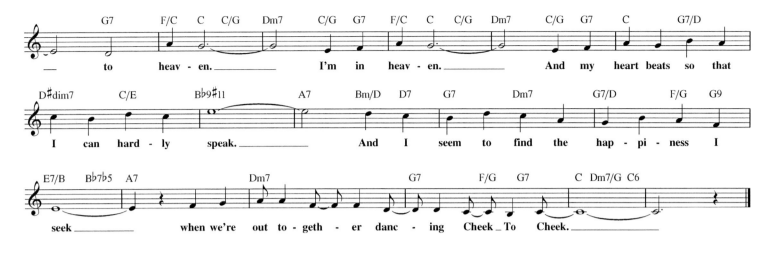

to heav - en. _____ I'm in heav - en. _____ And my heart beats so that

I can hard - ly speak. _____ And I seem to find the hap - pi - ness I

seek _____ when we're out to - geth - er danc - ing Cheek _ To Cheek. _____

CHERRY PINK AND APPLE BLOSSOM WHITE
from UNDERWATER

French Words by JACQUES LARUE
English Words by MACK DAVID
Music by MARCEL LOUIGUY

It's cher - ry pink and ap - ple blos - som white _ when your true lov - er comes your way. It's cher - ry pink and ap - ple

blos - som white _ the po - ets say. The sto - ry goes that once a cher - ry tree _

be - side an ap - ple tree did grow. And there a boy once met his bride to be _

long, long a - go. The boy looked in - to her eyes. It was a sight to en thrall, the breez - es

joined in their sighs. The blos - soms start - ed to fall. And as they gen - tly ca - ressed, the lov - ers

looked up to find the branch - es of the two trees were in - ter - twined. And that is why the po - ets

al - ways write, _ if there's a new moon bright a - bove, it's cher - ry pink and ap - ple

blos - som white _ when you're in love. It's cher - ry pink and ap - ple love. _____

CHIM CHIM CHER-EE
from Walt Disney's MARY POPPINS

Words and Music by RICHARD M. SHERMAN
and ROBERT B. SHERMAN

Lightly, with gusto

Chim chim-in-ey, chim chim-in-ey, chim chim cher-ee! A sweep is as luck-y, as

luck-y can be. Chim chim-in-ey, chim chim-in-ey, chim chim cher-oo! Good luck will rub

off when I shakes 'ands with you, or blow me a kiss and that's luck-y, too. *(Instrumental)*

Now, as the lad-der of life 'as been strung, you
I choose me bris-tles with pride, yes, I do: a

may think a sweep's on the bot-tom-most rung. Though I spends me time in the
broom for the shaft and a brush for the flue. Though I'm cov-ered with soot from me

ash-es and smoke, in this 'ole wide world there's no 'ap-pi-er bloke.
'ead to me toes, a sweep knows 'e's wel-come wher-ev-er 'e goes.

Up where the smoke is all bill-ered and curled, 'tween pave-ment and star, is the chim-ney sweep

world. When there's 'ard-ly no day nor 'ard-ly no night, there's things 'alf in

shad-ow and 'alf-way in light. On the roof-tops of Lon-don, coo, what a sight!

Chim chim-in-ey, chim chim-in-ey, chim chim cher-ee! When you're with a sweep you're in

glad com-pa-ny. No-where is there a more 'ap-pi-er crew than them wot sings,

"Chim chim cher-ee, chim cher-oo!" Chim chim-in-ey, chim chim, cher-ee, chim cher-oo!

CHINATOWN
from the Paramount Motion Picture CHINATOWN

Copyright © 1974 (Renewed 2002) by Ensign Music

Music by JERRY GOLDSMITH

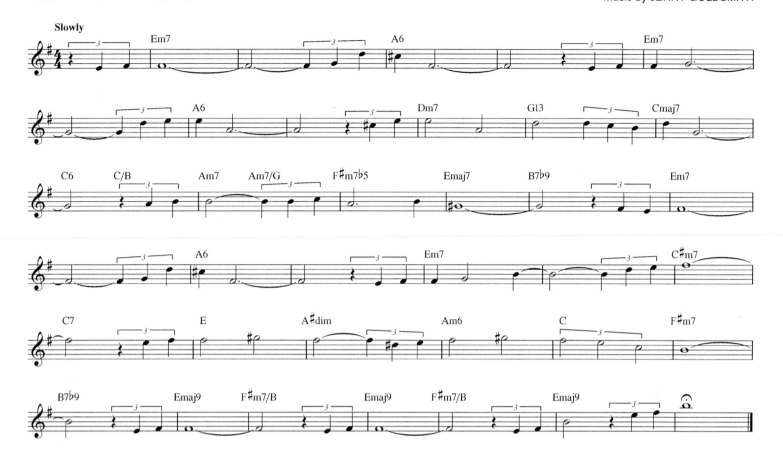

CINDERELLA
from Walt Disney's CINDERELLA

© 1948 Walt Disney Music Company
Copyright Renewed

Words and Music by MACK DAVID,
AL HOFFMAN and JERRY LIVINGSTON

CINEMA PARADISO
from CINEMA PARADISO

Music by ENNIO MORRICONE

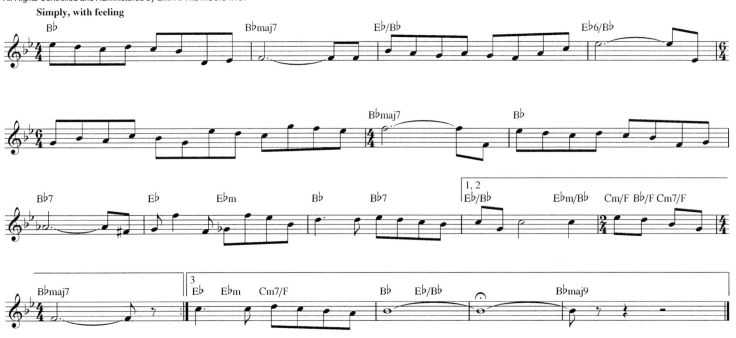

CIRCLE OF LIFE
from Walt Disney Pictures' THE LION KING

Music by ELTON JOHN
Lyrics by TIM RICE

COAL MINER'S DAUGHTER
from COAL MINER'S DAUGHTER

Words and Music by
LORETTA LYNN

COCKTAILS FOR TWO
from the Paramount Picture MURDER AT THE VANITIES

Words and Music by ARTHUR JOHNSTON
and SAM COSLOW

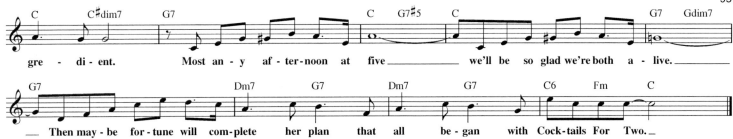

gre - di - ent.   Most an - y af - ter-noon at five _____ we'll be so glad we're both a - live. _____

_ Then may - be for - tune will com-plete her plan that all be - gan with Cock-tails For Two. _

COLE'S SONG
from MR. HOLLAND'S OPUS

Words by JULIAN LENNON and JUSTIN CLAYTON
Music by MICHAEL KAMEN

Slowly, with feeling

I feel that the love a - round me _ has come from an-oth - er world. I have

lost love, I have found love. From the mo - ment you were born I could see a new be -

gin - ning. _ Come _ to me, _ let me tell you how, how I've lost love and now I've

found love in a world of bro - ken dreams. I was wrong to de - ny your

feel - ings _ and I'm sor - ry _ if I've caused you _ pain. _ I was lost then, so con -

fused then, and I be - lieve that you would change that. There are bro - ken hearts we _ can

mend. Through the mu - sic we've _ learned to love _ a - gain. Through the sad notes, through the

years there were times when I just could-n't tell _____ you. And now we've come to an un - der -

stand - ing _ and I'm sor - ry ____ that it took so _ long. _ I have lost love, I have

found love from the mo - ment you were born. I have lost you and now I've found you. Let me

feel your heart, let me hear your song.

COLORS OF THE WIND
from Walt Disney's POCAHONTAS

Music by ALAN MENKEN
Lyrics by STEPHEN SCHWARTZ

COME SATURDAY MORNING
(Saturday Morning)
from the Paramount Picture THE STERILE CUCKOO

Words by DORY PREVIN
Music by FRED KARLIN

COME WHAT MAY
from the Motion Picture MOULIN ROUGE

Words and Music by
DAVID BAERWALD

Slowly

Male: Nev-er knew I could feel ___ like this, ___ like I've ___ nev-er seen ___ the sky ___

___ be - fore. Want to van - ish in - side ___ your kiss. ___

Ev - 'ry day ___ I love ___ you more and ___ more. Lis - ten to ___ my heart. ___ Can you

hear it sing and tell - ing me ___ to give ___ you ev - 'ry - thing?

Sea - sons ___ may change, ___ win - ter to spring, but I love you un - til the

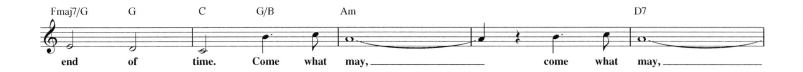

end of time. Come what may, _____ come what may, _____

___ I will love you un - til my dy - ing ___ day. _____

Female: Sud - den - ly the world ___ seems such a per - fect place. Sud - den - ly it moves with such ___ a

per - fect ___ grace. *Both:* Sud - den - ly my life does - n't seem _____ such a waste. ___

COMEDY TONIGHT
from A FUNNY THING HAPPENED ON THE WAY TO THE FORUM

Words and Music by
STEPHEN SONDHEIM

COMING TO AMERICA
from the Paramount Motion Picture COMING TO AMERICA

Words and Music by NILE RODGERS
and NANCY HUANG

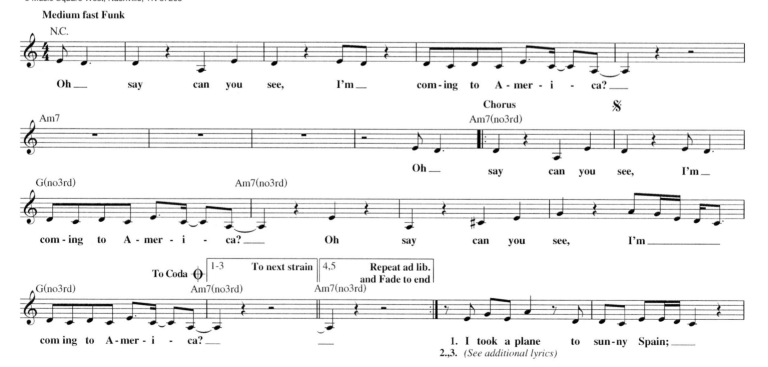

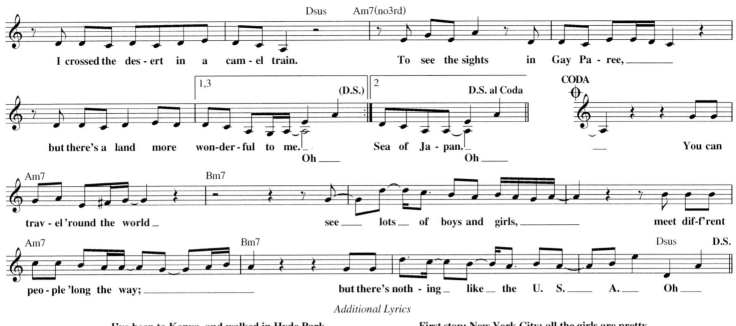

I crossed the des-ert in a cam-el train. To see the sights in Gay Pa-ree,___ but there's a land more won-der-ful to me. Sea of Ja-pan.___ You can trav-el 'round the world___ see___ lots___ of boys and girls,___ meet dif-f'rent peo-ple 'long the way;___ but there's noth-ing___ like___ the U. S. A.___ Oh___

Additional Lyrics

I've been to Kenya, and walked in Hyde Park,
Seen Copenhagen after dark with my baby.
I met the Pope at the Vatican,
Seen Ghana, Tijuana and the Sea of Japan.
Chorus

First stop: New York City; all the girls are pretty.
Next stop: Miami; everybody was jammin'.
I bought a ticket to L.A.; that's the perfect way.
Everybody in the world is coming to the U.S.A.
Chorus

CONSIDER YOURSELF
from the Columbia Pictures - Romulus Motion Picture Production of Lionel Bart's OLIVER!

Words and Music by LIONEL BART

Con - sid - er your-self___ at home,___ con - sid - er your-self___ one of the
sid - er your-self___ well in;___ con - sid - er your-self___ part of the

fam - i - ly___ We've tak - en to you___ so strong.___ It's
fur - ni - ture___ There is - n't a lot___ to spare;___ who

clear we're go - ing to get a - long! Con -
cares? What - ev - er we've got we share! If it should chance to be

we should see some hard - er days,___ emp - ty lard - er days,___ why grouse?___

___ Al - ways a chance we'll meet some-bod - y to foot the bill,___ then the drinks are

on the house!___ Con - sid - er your-self___ our mate.___

___ We don't want to have___ no fuss.___ For af - ter some con -

sid - er - a - tion, we can state: con - sid - er your-self___ one of us.

COULD I HAVE THIS DANCE
from URBAN COWBOY

Words and Music by WAYLAND HOLYFIELD
and BOB HOUSE

COUNT YOUR BLESSINGS INSTEAD OF SHEEP
from the Motion Picture Irving Berlin's WHITE CHRISTMAS

Words and Music by
IRVING BERLIN

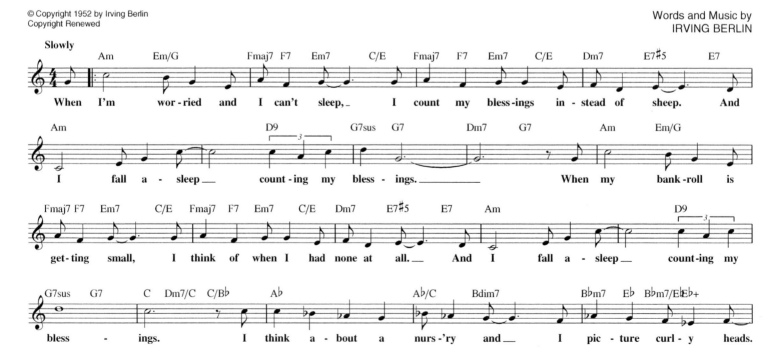

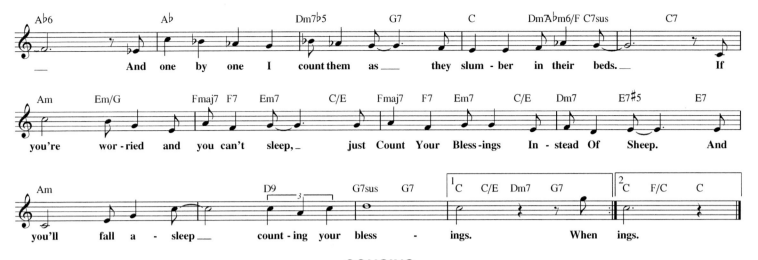

COUSINS
(Love Theme)
from the Paramount Picture COUSINS

Music by ANGELO BADALAMENTI

CRADLE OF LOVE

Words and Music by DAVID WERNER
and BILLY IDOL

CODA

ev-er I do _ ow, ow, ow. Rock the cra-dle of love, _____ yeah! Rock the cra-dle of love, _ ooh.

Sent from heav-en a-bove, _ that's right. She rocked the cra-dle of love. _____ Ow!

Rock the cra-dle of love, _ yeah. _ Cra - dle of love. _ That's me, ma - ma.

Repeat and Fade

I'll rob the dev-il of love. _ Al-right. Cra - dle of _ lo' - ove. Ow!

CRUELLA DE VIL
from Walt Disney's 101 DALMATIANS

Words and Music by
MEL LEVEN

Cru - el - la De Vil, _ Cru - el - la De Vil, _ if she does-n't scare _ you, no

e - vil thing will. _ To see her is to take a sud - den chill. _____ Cru -

el - la, Cru - el - la De Vil. The curl of her lips, _ the ice in her stare; _ all

in - no - cent chil - dren had bet - ter be - ware. _ She's like a spi - der wait - ing for the

kill. _____ Look out for Cru - el - la De Vil. At first you think Cru - el - la is the

dev - il, _____ but af - ter time has worn a - way the shock, _ you

come to re - a - lize _____ you've seen her kind of eyes _ watch - ing you from un - der - neath a

rock. This vam - pire _ bat, _ this in - hu - man beast, _ she

ought to be locked _ up and nev - er re - leased. _ The world was such a whole - some place un -

- til _____ Cru - el - la, Cru - el - la De Vil. Cru - Vil.

DANCING IN THE STREET
from the Paramount Motion Picture FOOTLOOSE

Words and Music by MARVIN GAYE,
IVY HUNTER and WILLIAM STEVENSON

DEARLY BELOVED
from YOU WERE NEVER LOVELIER

Music by JEROME KERN
Words by JOHNNY MERCER

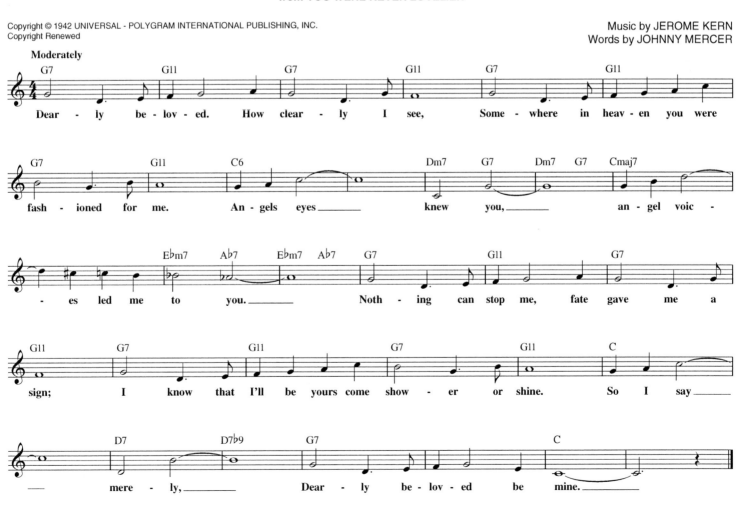

DANCING IN THE SHEETS
from the Paramount Motion Picture FOOTLOOSE

Music by BILL WOLFER
Words by DEAN PITCHFORD

With a driving beat

(Instrumental)

Play 4 times

I caught you smil - ing; I know I've seen you here be - fore.
We feel the rhy - thm; we've got the mu - sic on our side.

How come you're hid - ing? Hey, don't you want to hit the floor?
If we go with 'em, I bet we'll have a won - der - ful ride.

The place is crowd - ed, or may - be you don't like the beat. ____
Your hands are cold, so may - be we can make some heat. ____

I've got a two - track play - ing in ___ my head, so let me take you some - where
Love is al - ways born on a chance, ___ so wrap a - round me and,

else in - stead. ___ Danc - ing in ___ the sheets. ____
ba - by, dance. ___

Grab your coat and wave good - bye to your friends. _ I want to take you where the

night nev - er ends. _ I feel the need to sweep you off of your feet. _ You and me, we should be

To Coda

danc - ing in the sheets; ____ danc - ing in ___ the sheets. ____

D.S.

(Instrumental)

D.S.S. al Coda

CODA

Repeat ad lib. and Fade

Danc - ing in ___ the sheets. ___

DANGER ZONE
from the Motion Picture TOP GUN

Words and Music by GIORGIO MORODER
and TOM WHITLOCK

Additional Lyrics

3. Out along the edge is always where I burn to be.
   The further on the edge, the hotter the intensity.
   To Coda

DAWN
from PRIDE AND PREJUDICE

By DARIO MARIANELLI

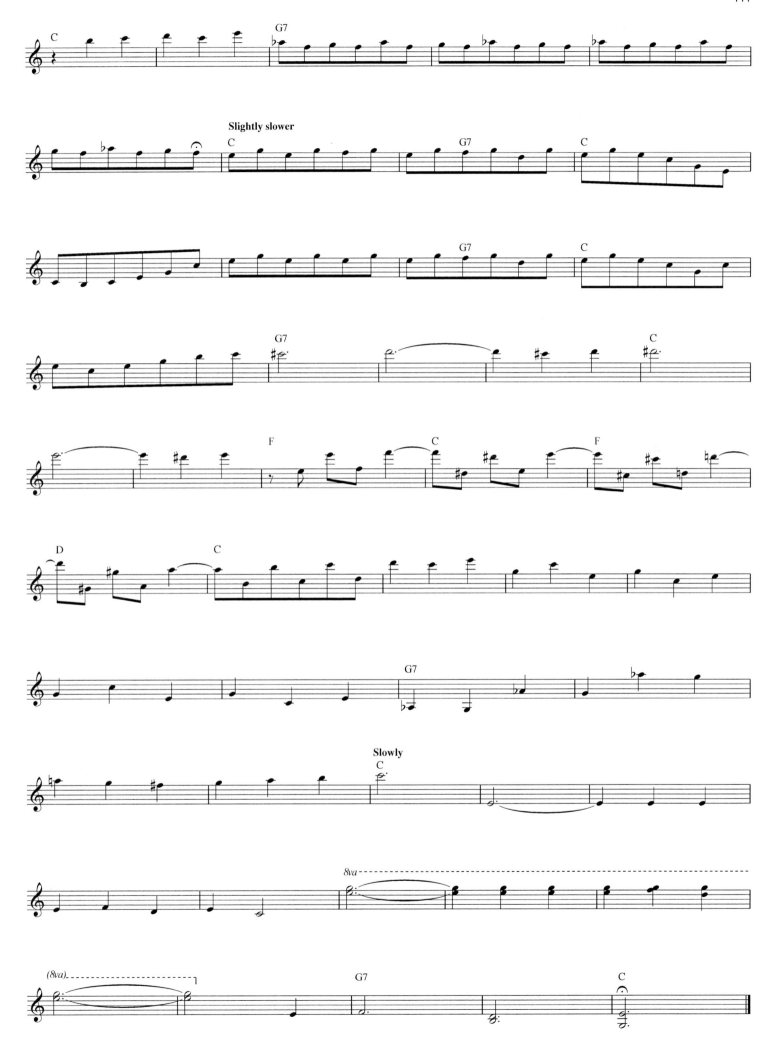

THE DAY I FALL IN LOVE
Love Theme from BEETHOVEN'S 2ND

Words and Music by CAROLE BAYER SAGER,
JAMES INGRAM and CLIF MAGNESS

DEEP IN THE HEART OF TEXAS

Words by JUNE HERSHEY
Music by DON SWANDER

DAY-O
(The Banana Boat Song)

Words and Music by IRVING BURGIE
and WILLIAM ATTAWAY

DIAMONDS ARE A GIRL'S BEST FRIEND

Words by LEO ROBIN
Music by JULE STYNE

DOLORES

from the Paramount Picture LAS VEGAS NIGHTS

Words by FRANK LOESSER
Music by LOUIS ALTER

DO YOU KNOW WHERE YOU'RE GOING TO?
Theme from MAHOGANY

Words by GERRY GOFFIN
Music by MICHAEL MASSER

Do you know where you're going to? Do you like the things that life is showing you? Where are you going to? Do you know?

Do you get what you're hoping for? When you look behind you there's no open door. What are you hoping for, do you know? Once we were standing still in time, chasing the fantasies that filled our minds. And you knew how I love you but my spirit was free, laughing at the questions that you once asked of me.

Do you know where you're going to? Do you like the things that life is showing you? Where are you going to, do you know? (Instrumental)

Now looking back at all we planned, we let so many dreams just slip through our hands. Why must we wait so long before we see, how sad the answers to those questions can be.

CODA

know? (Instrumental)

DRIVING MISS DAISY
from DRIVING MISS DAISY

By HANS ZIMMER

118

DOMINIQUE
from THE SINGING NUN

© 1962, 1963 (Renewed 1990, 1991) INTERSONG PRIMAVERA, N.V.
All Rights for the U.S. Controlled and Administered by COLGEMS-EMI MUSIC INC.

English Lyrics and Arrangement by NOEL REGNEY
By SOEUR SOURIRE, O.P.

DON'T CRY FOR ME ARGENTINA
from EVITA

© Copyright 1976, 1977 EVITA MUSIC LTD.
Copyright Renewed
All Rights for the United States and Canada Controlled and Administered by
UNIVERSAL MUSIC CORP.

Words by TIM RICE
Music by ANDREW LLOYD WEBBER

DON'T RAIN ON MY PARADE
from FUNNY GIRL

Words by BOB MERRILL
Music by JULE STYNE

A DREAM IS A WISH YOUR HEART MAKES
from Walt Disney's CINDERELLA

Words and Music by MACK DAVID,
AL HOFFMAN and JERRY LIVINGSTON

DON'T WORRY, BE HAPPY

featured in the Motion Picture COCKTAIL

Words and Music by
BOBBY McFERRIN

Additional Lyrics
Spoken ad lib. over repeat and fade:
Don't worry. Don't worry. Don't do it.
Be happy. Put a smile on your face.
Don't bring everybody down. Don't
Worry. It will soon pass, whatever it is.
Don't worry. Be happy. I'm not worried.
I'm happy.

THE DREAME
from SENSE AND SENSIBILITY

By PATRICK DOYLE

DON'T YOU (FORGET ABOUT ME)
from the Universal Picture THE BREAKFAST CLUB

Words and Music by KEITH FORSEY
and STEVE SCHIFF

Moderately, with a steady beat

1. Won't you come see a-bout me, ___ I'll be a-lone ___ danc-ing, you know it, ba-by.
2. (*See additional lyrics*)

Tell me your trou-bles and doubts, ___ giv-en ev-'ry-thing in-side and out.

Love's strange, so real in the dark, ___ Think of the ten-der things that we were work-ing on.

Slow chains may pull us a-part ___ when our life ___ gets in-to your heart, ___ ba-by.

Don't you for-get a-bout me. ___ Don't, don't, don't, don't.

Don't you for-get a-bout me. ___ | Will you stand a-bove ___ me, ___ / Will you rec-og-nize ___ me, ___

Look my way, ___ nev-er love ___ me.) Rain keeps fall-ing, rain keeps fall-ing
Call my name ___ or walk on by? ___)
As you walk on by? ___

down, ___ down, ___ down. ___ ___ down, ___ down. **D.C. al Coda**

CODA
But you walk on by, _
As you walk on by, _

Will you call my name? ___ When you walk a-way, ___
Will you call my name? ___ Or will you walk a-way?

Will you walk on by? Come on and call my name. _

Additional Lyrics

2. Don't you try and pretend,
It's my feeling, we'll win in the end.
I won't harm you, or touch your defenses,
Vanity, insecurity.
Don't you forget about me,
I'll be alone dancing, you know it, baby.
Going to take you apart,
I'll put us back together at heart, baby.

Don't you forget about me,
Don't, don't, don't, don't.
Don't you forget about me. (*To Coda*)

EASTER PARADE

featured in the Motion Picture Irving Berlin's EASTER PARADE
from AS THOUSANDS CHEER

Words and Music by
IRVING BERLIN

DREAMS TO DREAM
(Finale Version)
from the Universal Motion Picture AN AMERICAN TAIL: FIEVEL GOES WEST

Words and Music by JAMES HORNER
and WILL JENNINGS

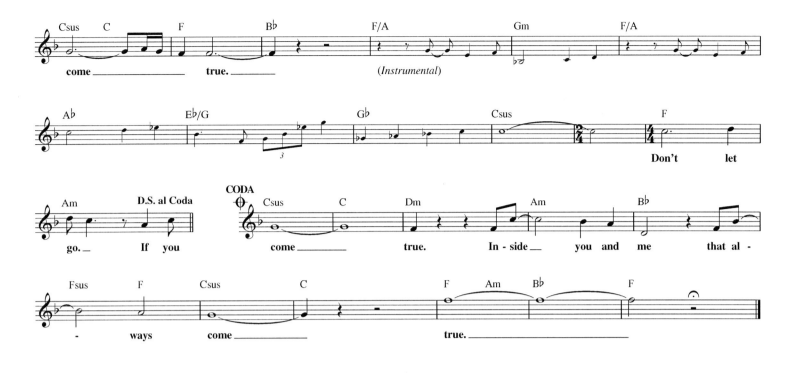

EASY TO LOVE
(You'd Be So Easy to Love)
from BORN TO DANCE

Words and Music by
COLE PORTER

END OF THE ROAD
from the Paramount Motion Picture BOOMERANG

Words and Music by BABYFACE,
L.A. REID and DARYL SIMMONS

Moderately

1. We be-long to-geth-er and you know that I'm right, __ Why do you play with my heart? Why
2. Girl, I know you real-ly love me, you just don't re-al-ize. ___ You've nev-er been there be-fore, it's
3. (*See additional lyrics*)

do you play with my mind? _____ You said we'd be for-ev-er said it'd nev-er die. ___
on-ly your first time. _____ May-be I'll for-give you, may-be you'll __ try. ___

How could you love me and leave me and nev-er say good-bye? Well, I
We should be hap-py to-geth-er, for-ev-er, you and I. Could you

can't sleep at night with-out hold-ing you tight. Girl, each time I try I just break down and cry.
love me a-gain like you loved me be-fore? This time, I want you to love me much more.

(1) Pain in my head, oh, I'd rath-er be dead, spin-nin' a-round and a-round. __ Al-though we've
(2,3) This time, in-stead just come back to my bed and, ba-by, just don't let me down. __

come to the end of the road, __ still I can't let __ you go. __ It's un-nat-ur-al. You be-

long to me, I be-long to you. __ Come to the end of the road, __ still I can't let __ you

go. __ It's un-nat-ur-al. You be-long to me, I be-long to you, __ oh.

To Coda
1, 2

3
long to me, I be-long to you. Al-though we've

D.S. al Coda

CODA
long to me, I be-long to you. __

Additional Lyrics

(*Spoken:*) Girl, I'm here for you.
All those times at night when you just hurt me,
And just ran out with that other fellow,
Baby, I know about it.
I just didn't care.
You just don't understand how much I love you, do you?
I'm here for you.
I'm not one to go out there and cheat all night just like you did, baby.
But that's alright, huh, I love you anyway.
And I'm still gonna be here for you 'til my dyin' day, baby.
Right now, I'm just in so much pain, baby.
'Cause you just won't come back to me, will you?

ENDLESS LOVE
from ENDLESS LOVE

Words and Music by
LIONEL RICHIE

EMPTY SADDLES
from RHYTHM ON THE RANGE

By BILLY HILL

Emp - ty sad - dles in the old cor - ral, Where do you ride to - night? Are ya round - in' up the do - gies, The
Emp - ty sad - dles in the old cor - ral, Where do you ride to - night? Are there rus - tlers on the bor - der or a

strays of long a - go; Are ya on the trail of buf - fa - lo?
band of Nav - a - jo; Are ya head - in' for the Al - a - mo? Emp - ty guns, cov - ered with rust,

Where do ya talk to - night? Emp - ty boots, cov - ered with dust, Where do ya walk to -

night? _____ Emp - ty sad - dles in the old cor - ral, My tears would be dried to - night; If you'll

on - ly say I'm lone - ly As ya car - ry my old pal, Emp - ty sad - dles in the old cor - ral.

THE ENGLISH PATIENT
from THE ENGLISH PATIENT

Written by GABRIEL YARED

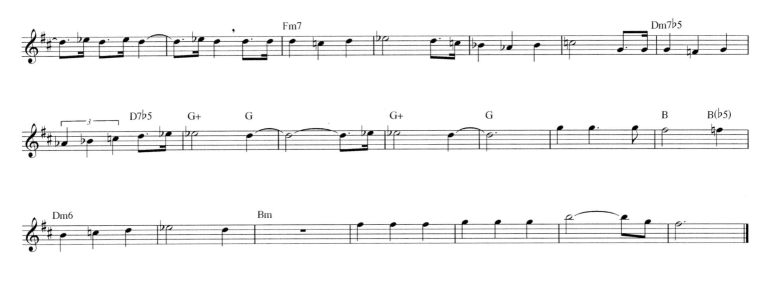

THE ENTERTAINER
featured in the Motion Picture THE STING

By SCOTT JOPLIN

THEME FROM "E.T. (THE EXTRA-TERRESTRIAL)"

from the Universal Picture E.T. (THE EXTRA-TERRESTRIAL)

Music by JOHN WILLIAMS

Majestically

EVERY ROAD LEADS BACK TO YOU
featured in the Motion Picture FOR THE BOYS

Words and Music by
DIANE WARREN

Moderate Ballad

Old friend, __ here we are, af-ter all the years and tears __ and all ____ that we've __ been __ through.
Old friend, __ there were times I did-n't want to see your face __ or hear __ your name __ a - gain.

It feels __ so good __ to see you. Look - ing __ back in time, there've been oth - er
Now those times are far ____ be - hind me. It's so good to see your smile, I'd for - got - ten

friends and oth - er lov - ers, but __ no ____ oth - er one __ like __ you.
how no - bod - y else ____ could make __ me smile the way __ you __ do.

All _____ my ____ life, _____ no one ev - er has known __ me bet - ter. __
All _____ this ____ time, _____ you're the one I still want ____ be - side __ me. __

I must have trav - eled down __ a thou - sand roads, ____ been so man-y plac - es, seen so man-y

fac - es, al - ways on my way to some - thing new. ____ But it does - n't mat - ter 'cause no

mat - ter where __ I go, _____ ev -'ry road leads back, ____ ev -'ry road just seems __ to

1. lead me __ back to you.

2. you. D.S. al Coda

CODA

road just seems __ to lead me __ back. Ev -'ry road ____ leads back, _____ ev -'ry

road just seems __ to lead me __ back to you. Ev -'ry road just seems __ to

lead me __ back to you.

EVERYBODY'S TALKIN'
(Echoes)
from MIDNIGHT COWBOY

Words and Music by
FRED NEIL

(EVERYTHING I DO) I DO IT FOR YOU
from the Motion Picture ROBIN HOOD: PRINCE OF THIEVES

Words and Music by BRYAN ADAMS,
R.J. LANGE and MICHAEL KAMEN

EXHALE
(Shoop Shoop)
from the Original Soundtrack Album WAITING TO EXHALE

Words and Music by
BABYFACE

THE EXODUS SONG
from EXODUS

Words by PAT BOONE
Music by ERNEST GOLD

EYE OF THE TIGER
Theme from ROCKY III

Words and Music by FRANK SULLIVAN
and JIM PETERIK

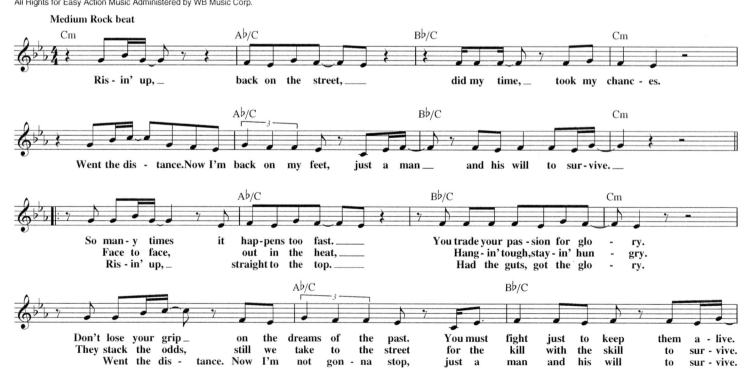

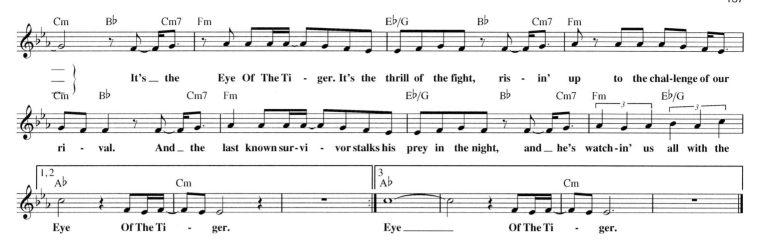

FAR AND AWAY
(Main Theme)
from the Universal Motion Picture FAR AND AWAY

Composed by JOHN WILLIAMS

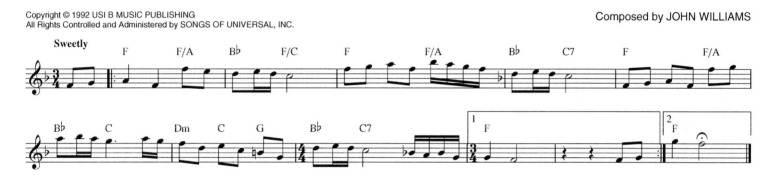

THEME FROM "FATAL ATTRACTION"
from the Paramount Motion Picture FATAL ATTRACTION

Music by MAURICE JARRE

FEED THE BIRDS
from Walt Disney's MARY POPPINS

Words and Music by RICHARD M. SHERMAN
and ROBERT B. SHERMAN

Moderately

Feed ___ the birds, tup-pence ___ a bag, Tup-pence, ___ tup-pence, ___ tup-pence ___ a bag.

"Feed ___ the birds," that's what she cries While o-ver-head her birds fill the skies. All a-

round the ca-the-dral the saints and a-pos-tles Look down as she sells her wares. ___ Al-

though you can't see it, you know they are smil-ing Each time some-one shows that he cares. ___

Though ___ her words are sim-ple ___ and few, Lis-ten, ___ lis-ten ___ she's call-ing to you.

Feed ___ the birds, tup-pence a bag, Tup-pence, ___ tup-pence, ___ tup-pence a bag.

A FINE ROMANCE
from SWING TIME

Words by DOROTHY FIELDS
Music by JEROME KERN

Moderately

A fine ro-mance! With no kiss-es! A fine ro-mance, my friend, this is! We
fine ro-mance! My good fel-low! You take ro-mance, I'll take jel-lo! You're

should be like a cou-ple of hot to-ma-toes, ___ but you're as cold as yes-ter-day's mashed po-
calm-er than the seal in the Arc-tic O-cean. ___ At least they flap their fins to ex-press e-

ta-toes. ___ A fine ro-mance! You won't nes-tle. A fine
mo-tion. ___ A fine ro-mance! With no quar-rels. With no

ro - mance.   You won't   wres - tle!   I   might as   well play   bridge with my old   maid aunts!
in - sults,   and all   mor - als!   I've nev - er mussed the   crease in your blue serge pants!

F   D7♭9   C   G7   1 C   2 C6

I have-n't got   a   chance.   This is   a fine ro - mance.   A
I nev-er get the chance. This is   a fine ro -   mance. _____

THE FIRM – MAIN TITLE
from the Paramount Motion Picture THE FIRM

Copyright © 1993 by Ensign Music

By DAVE GRUSIN

Moderately

LOVE THEME FROM "FLASHDANCE"
from the Paramount Picture FLASHDANCE

Music by
GIORGIO MORODER

FLASHDANCE...WHAT A FEELING
from the Paramount Picture FLASHDANCE

Lyrics by KEITH FORSEY and IRENE CARA
Music by GIORGIO MORODER

FLY LIKE AN EAGLE
featured in the Motion Picture SPACE JAM

Words and Music by
STEVE MILLER

THE FOLKS WHO LIVE ON THE HILL
from HIGH, WIDE AND HANDSOME

Lyrics by OSCAR HAMMERSTEIN II
Music by JEROME KERN

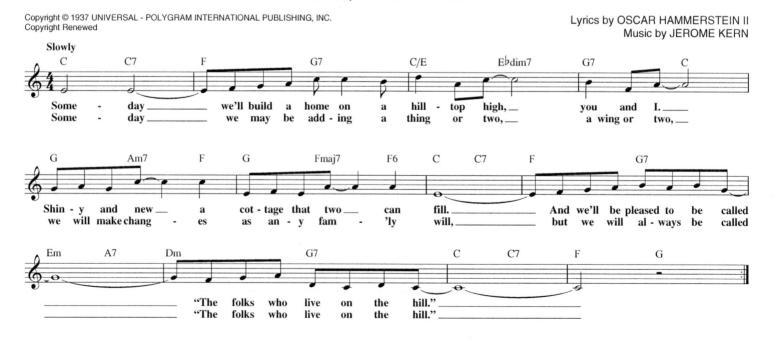

FOR ALL WE KNOW
from the Motion Picture LOVERS AND OTHER STRANGERS

Words by ROBB WILSON and ARTHUR JAMES
Music by FRED KARLIN

FOOTLOOSE
Theme from the Paramount Motion Picture FOOTLOOSE

Words by DEAN PITCHFORD and KENNY LOGGINS
Music by KENNY LOGGINS

Fast Rock and Roll

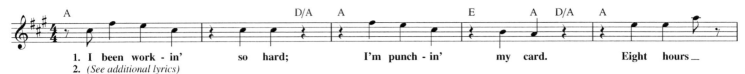

1. I been work - in' so hard; I'm punch - in' my card. Eight hours __
2. (See additional lyrics)

for what? Oh, tell me what I got. I've got this feel - in',

that time's just hold - in' me down. __ I'll hit the ceil - in', __ or else I'll

tear up this town. __ **CHORUS** To - night I got - ta cut loose, foot -

loose; kick off your Sun - day shoes. Please, Lou - ise, pull me off __ of my

knees. Jack, get back; come on be - fore we crack.

Lose your blues, ev - 'ry - bod - y cut Foot - loose. loose.

Additional Lyrics

2. You're playin' so cool
Obeying every rule
Did way down in your heart
You're burnin', yearnin' for some...
Somebody to tell you
That life ain't a-passin' you by.
I'm tryin' to tell you
It will if you don't evey try;
You can fly if you'd only cut...
Chorus

Chorus:
Loose, Footloose;
Kick off your Sunday shoes.
Ooh-ee, Marie,
Shake it, shake it for me.
Whoa, Milo;
Come on, come on let's go.
Lose your blues,
Everybody cut Footloose.

FOR THE FIRST TIME
from ONE FINE DAY

Words and Music by JAMES NEWTON HOWARD,
JUD FRIEDMAN and ALLAN RICH

FORREST GUMP – MAIN TITLE
(Feather Theme)
from the Paramount Motion Picture FORREST GUMP

Music by
ALAN SILVESTRI

FOUR WEDDINGS AND A FUNERAL/FUNERAL BLUES

from FOUR WEDDINGS AND A FUNERAL

By RICHARD BENNETT

FRIEND LIKE ME
from Walt Disney's ALADDIN

Lyrics by HOWARD ASHMAN
Music by ALAN MENKEN

FRIENDLY PERSUASION
from the Motion Picture FRIENDLY PERSUASION

Words by PAUL FRANCIS WEBSTER
Music by DIMITRI TIOMKIN

THE FRIENDSHIP THEME
from Touchstone Pictures' BEACHES

Music by GEORGES DELERUE

FRIGHT NIGHT

Words and Music by
JOE LAMONT

FROM HERE TO ETERNITY

from FROM HERE TO ETERNITY

Words by ROBERT WELLS
Music by FRED KARGER

Moderately

You vowed your love, _____ from here to e - ter - ni - ty, _____ a

love so true, _____ it nev - er would die. _____ You

gave your lips, _____ gave them so will - ing - ly. _____ How

could I know _____ your kiss meant good - bye? Now

I'm a - lone, _____ with on - ly a mem - o - ry. _____ My

emp - ty arms _____ will nev - er know why. Though

you are gone, _____ this love that you left with me, _____ will

live from here to e - ter - ni - ty.

FUNNY GIRL

from FUNNY GIRL

Words by BOB MERRILL
Music by JULE STYNE

Modeately slow

Fun - ny, did ya hear that? Fun - ny! Yes, that guy said: "Hon - ey,

you're a fun - ny girl!" _____ That's me, _ I just keep them in stitch - es,

dou - bled in half. _____ And tho' I may be all wrong for the guy, _ I'm good for a laugh.

_ I guess it's not fun - ny, Life is far from sun - ny, When the laugh is o - ver,

And the joke's on you. _____ A girl ought to have a sense of hu - mor, that's

one thing you real - ly need for sure when you're a fun - ny girl, the fel - low said "A

fun - ny girl." Fun - ny, how it ain't so fun - ny, fun - ny girl. _____

GALE'S THEME
(Main Title)
from THE RIVER WILD

By JERRY GOLDSMITH

GEORGY GIRL
from GEORGY GIRL

Words by JIM DALE
Music by TOM SPRINGFIELD

Hey, there! Geor-gy Girl, swing-ing down the street so fan-cy-free. No-bod-y you meet could ev-er see the lone-li-ness there in-side you. Hey there! Geor-gy Girl.

Why do all the boys just pass you by? Could it be you just don't try, or is it the
Dream-ing of the some-one you could be. Life is a re-al-i-ty, you can't al-ways

clothes you wear? You're al-ways win-dow shop-ping but
run a-way. Don't be so scared of chang-ing and

nev-er stop-ping to buy. So shed those dow-dy feath-ers and fly
re-ar-rang-ing your-self. It's time for jump-ing down from the shelf

a lit-tle bit. Hey there! Geor-gy Girl, there's an-oth-er Geor-gy deep in-side.

Bring out all the love you hide and oh, what a change there'd be. The world would see

a new Geor-gy Girl. Girl. A new Geor-gy

GET HAPPY
from SUMMER STOCK
from the Musical Production NINE-FIFTEEN REVUE

Lyric by TED KOEHLER
Music by HAROLD ARLEN

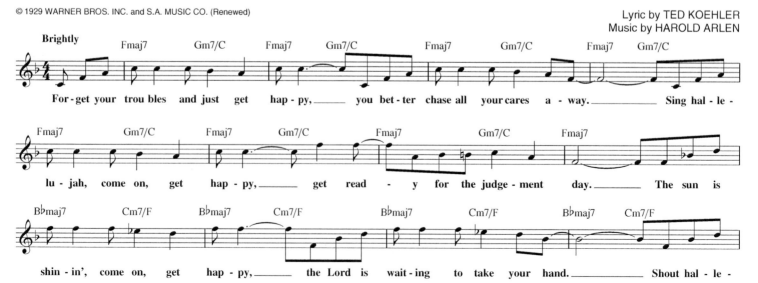

For-get your trou-bles and just get hap-py, you bet-ter chase all your cares a-way. Sing hal-le-

lu-jah, come on, get hap-py, get read-y for the judge-ment day. The sun is

shin-in', come on, get hap-py, the Lord is wait-ing to take your hand. Shout hal-le-

GIGI
from GIGI

Words by ALAN JAY LERNER
Music by FREDERICK LOEWE

GHOST
Theme from the Paramount Motion Picture GHOST

By MAURICE JARRE

Flowing and expressively

THE GIRL FROM IPANEMA
(Garôta de Ipanema)
from THE COLOR OF MONEY

Music by ANTONIO CARLOS JOBIM
English Words by NORMAN GIMBEL
Original Words by VINICIUS DE MORAES

Moderate Bossa Nova

Tall and tan and young and love-ly, the girl from I-pa-ne-
When she walks she's like a sam-ba that swings so cool and sways

-ma goes walk-ing, and when she pass-es, each one she pass-es goes
so gen-tle, that when she pass-es, each one she pass-es goes

"a-a-h"
"a-a-h"
Oh, but I watch her so

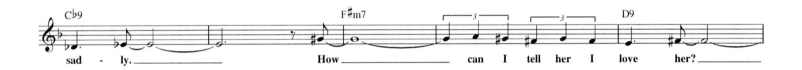

sad-ly. How can I tell her I love her?

Yes, I would give my heart glad-ly, but each

day when she walks to the sea, she looks straight a-head not at me. Tall and tan and young

and love-ly, the girl from I-pa-ne-ma goes walk-ing, and when she pass-es I smile,

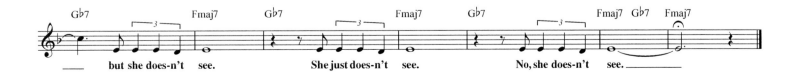

but she does-n't see. She just does-n't see. No, she does-n't see.

GIRL TALK
from the Paramount Picture HARLOW

Words by BOBBY TROUP
Music by NEAL HEFTI

GIVE A LITTLE WHISTLE
from Walt Disney's PINOCCHIO

Words by NED WASHINGTON
Music by LEIGH HARLINE

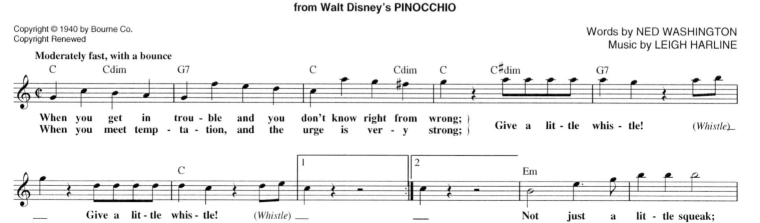

Puck - er up and blow. And if your whis - tle's weak; yell "Jim - i - ny Crick - et."

Take the straight and nar - row path and if you start to slide; Give a lit - tle whis - tle! *(Whistle)* Give a lit - tle

whis - tle! *(Whistle)* And al - ways let your con science be your guide.

THE GLORY OF LOVE
from GUESS WHO'S COMING TO DINNER
featured in the Motion Picture BEACHES

Words and Music by
BILLY HILL

You've got to give a lit - tle, take a lit - tle and let your poor heart break a lit - tle

that's the sto - ry of, that's the glo - ry of love. You've got to laugh a lit - tle

cry a lit - tle before the clouds roll by a lit - tle that's the sto - ry of, that's the glo - ry of

love. As long as there's the two of us we've got the world and all its

charms. And when the world is through with us we've got each oth - er's arms. You've got to

win a lit - tle, lose a lit - tle and al - ways have the blues a lit - tle. That's the sto - ry of,

that's the glo - ry of love. You've got to love.

GO THE DISTANCE
from Walt Disney Pictures' HERCULES

Music by ALAN MENKEN
Lyrics by DAVID ZIPPEL

GOD BLESS' THE CHILD

Words and Music by ARTHUR HERZOG JR.
and BILLIE HOLIDAY

GOD HELP THE OUTCASTS
from Walt Disney's THE HUNCHBACK OF NOTRE DAME

Music by ALAN MENKEN
Lyrics by STEPHEN SCHWARTZ

seek - ing an an - swer to why they were born. Winds of mis - for - tune have blown them a - bout. You made the out - casts; don't cast them out. The poor and un - luck - y, the weak and the odd; I thought we all were the chil - dren of God.

(Instrumental)

GODFATHER II
Theme from the Paramount Picture GODFATHER II

By NINO ROTA

Slowly

THE GODFATHER WALTZ
from the Paramount Picture THE GODFATHER, GODFATHER II, and GODFATHER III

by NINO ROTA

GOLDEN EARRINGS
from the Paramount Picture GOLDEN EARRINGS

Words by JAY LIVINGSTON and RAY EVANS
Music by VICTOR YOUNG

GOOD LOVIN'
featured in the Motion Picture THE BIG CHILL

Words and Music by RUDY CLARK
and ART RESNICK

GOOD MORNING
from SINGIN' IN THE RAIN

Words by ARTHUR FREED
Music by NACIO HERB BROWN

THEME FROM "GOODBYE, COLUMBUS"
from the Paramount Picture GOODBYE, COLUMBUS

Words and Music by
JAMES YESTER

THE GREEN LEAVES OF SUMMER

Words by PAUL FRANCIS WEBSTER
Music by DIMITRI TIOMKIN

THE GUNS OF NAVARONE
from THE GUNS OF NAVARONE

Words and Music by DIMITRI TIOMKIN
and PAUL WEBSTER

A GUY WHAT TAKES HIS TIME
from SHE DONE HIM WRONG

Words and Music by
RALPH RAINGER

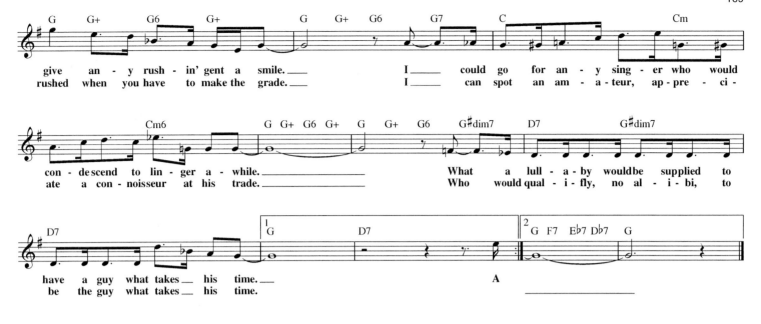

HANDS OF TIME
Theme from the Screen Gems Television Production BRIAN'S SONG

Words by ALAN and MARILYN BERGMAN
Music by MICHEL LEGRAND

HAKUNA MATATA
from Walt Disney Pictures' THE LION KING

Music by ELTON JOHN
Lyrics by TIM RICE

HAPPY HOLIDAY
from the Motion Picture Irving Berlin's HOLIDAY INN

Words and Music by
IRVING BERLIN

A HARD DAY'S NIGHT
from A HARD DAY'S NIGHT

Words and Music by JOHN LENNON
and PAUL McCARTNEY

D.S. al Coda
(Verse 1)

Bm · · · · G · Em · · · · C · D

right. When I'm home feel-ing you hold - ing me tight, tight, yeah. It's been a

CODA · G · C9 · G · C · F(add9) · Repeat and Fade

You know I feel al - right, you know I feel al - right. (Instrumenal)

HEART AND SOUL
from the Paramount Short Subject A SONG IS BORN

Words by FRANK LOESSER
Music by HOAGY CARMICHAEL

Moderately, lightly rhythmical

F · Dm7 · Gm7 · C7 · F · Dm7 · Gm7 · C7 · F · Dm

Heart and soul I fell in love with you. Heart and soul the way a fool would do, mad - ly

Gm · C7 · F · Dm7 · Gm7 · C7 · F · Dm7 · Gm7 · C7

be cause you held me tight and stole a kiss in the night. Heart and soul I begged to be a dored.

F · Dm7 · Gm7 · C7 · F · Dm · Gm · C7 · F

Lost con - trol and tum bled o - ver board, glad - ly that mag - ic night we kissed there in the

F7 · Bb · A7 · D7 · G7 · C7 · F7 · E7 · A7 · Bb · A7

moon- mist. Oh! but your lips were thrill - ing, much too thrill - ing. Nev- er be- fore were

D7 · G7 · C7 · F7 · E7 · C7 · F · Dm7 · Gm7 · C7 · F · Dm7

mine so strange - ly will - ing. But now I see what one embrace can do. Look at me,

Gm7 · C7 · F · Dm · Gm7 · C7 · A7 · D7

it's got me lov - ing you mad - ly, that lit - tle kiss you stole

Gm · G9 · C7 · 1. F · Dm7 · Gm7 · C7 · 2. F · Dm7 · Gm7 · C7b9 · F

held all my heart and soul. soul.

THE HEAT IS ON
from the Paramount Picture BEVERLY HILLS COP

Words by KEITH FORSEY
Music by HAROLD FALTERMEYER

HEAVEN CAN WAIT
(Love Theme)
from the Paramount Motion Picture HEAVEN CAN WAIT

Music by DAVE GRUSIN

HEIGH-HO
The Dwarfs' Marching Song from Walt Disney's SNOW WHITE AND THE SEVEN DWARFS

Words by LARRY MOREY
Music by FRANK CHURCHILL

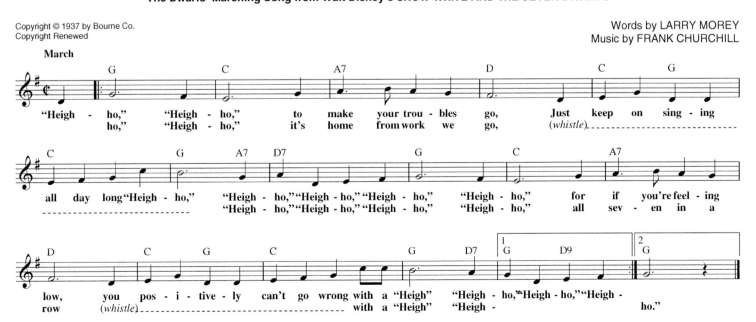

HELLO AGAIN

from the Motion Picture THE JAZZ SINGER

Words by NEIL DIAMOND
Music by NEIL DIAMOND and ALAN LINDGREN

Moderately slow

Hel - lo a - gain, hel - lo. Just called to say 'hel - lo'. I could - n't sleep at

all to - night. And I know it's late, but I could - n't wait. Hel - lo, my friend, hel -

lo. Just called to let you know I think a - bout you ev - 'ry night when I'm

here a - lone and you're there at home. Hel - lo. May - be it's been cra - zy,

and may - be I'm to blame, but I put my heart a - bove my head.

We've been through it all, and you loved me just the same. And when you're not there, I

just need to hear: Hel - lo, my friend, hel - lo. It's good to need you so. It's

good to love you like I do and to feel this way when I hear you say 'hel -

lo'. Hel - lo, my friend, hel - lo. Just

called to let you know I think a - bout you ev - 'ry night. And I

know it's late, but I could - n't wait. Hel - lo.

HIGH HOPES

Words by SAMMY CAHN
Music by JAMES VAN HEUSEN

HELP!
from HELP!

Words and Music by JOHN LENNON
and PAUL McCARTNEY

HIGH NOON
(Do Not Forsake Me)
from HIGH NOON

Words and Music by DIMITRI TIOMKIN
and NED WASHINGTON

HIT THE ROAD TO DREAMLAND

from the Paramount Picture STAR SPANGLED RHYTHM
from L.A. CONFIDENTIAL

Words by JOHNNY MERCER
Music by HAROLD ARLEN

HOLDING OUT FOR A HERO
from the Paramount Motion Picture FOOTLOOSE

Words by DEAN PITCHFORD
Music by JIM STEINMAN

HOPELESSLY DEVOTED TO YOU
from GREASE

Words and Music by
JOHN FARRAR

Guess mine is not the first ____ heart bro - ken.   My eyes are not the first ____ to
know I'm just a fool ____ who's will - in' ____   to sit a - round and wait ____ for
head is say - in', "Fool, ____ for - get him."   My heart is say - in', "Don't ____ let

cry.   I'm not the ___ first to know   there's just no ___ get - tin' o - ver
you.   But, ba - by, ___ can't you see   there's noth - in' else for me ____ to
go.   Hold on ___ to the end."   And that's what ___ I in - tend ____ to

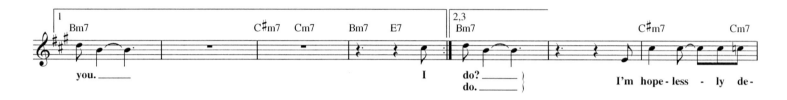

you. _____   I   do? _____ }
do. _____ }   I'm hope - less - ly de -

vot - ed ____ to you.   But now there's no - where to hide ____ since you

pushed my love a - side. ____   I'm out ____ of my head,   hope - less - ly de - vot - ed ____ to

you, _____   hope - less - ly de - vot - ted ____ to you. _____

To Coda ⊕

D.S. al Coda
(take 2nd ending)

Hope - less - ly de - vot - ed ____ to you. _____   My

CODA ⊕

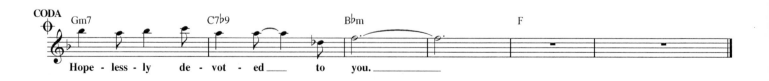

Hope - less - ly de - vot - ed ____ to you. _____

HOW DEEP IS YOUR LOVE
from the Motion Picture SATURDAY NIGHT FEVER

Words and Music by BARRY GIBB,
ROBIN GIBB and MAURICE GIBB

HOW LUCKY CAN YOU GET
from FUNNY LADY

Words by FRED EBB
Music by JOHN KANDER

Moderately

Ba-do - di-o - di-o - di ain't we got fun; ___ and what is more we got the blues on the run. ___

Sa - tin on my shoul-ders and a smile on my lips. ___ How luck-y can you get? And I got
Ev - 'ry time I roll the dice the sev-en comes up. ___ How luck-y can you get? This

mon - ey in my pock-ets and at my fin-ger - tips. ___ How luck-y can you get? Ev-
bowl of punch is ver-y nice, I'll pour you a cup. ___ How luck-y can you get? If ___

- 'ry night a par-ty where the fun nev-er ends; ___ you can cir-cle the world with our cir-cle of friends. When I'm
___ you care to join us we will al-ways say "yes;" ___ if you look in the book you will find our ad-dress.

mak-in' mer-ry mu-sic with this part-ner of mine, ___ we're a per-fect du-et. ___
There's no need to tel-e-phone, just come as you are, ___ take a train ___ or a jet. ___

Wow, how luck-y can you get? (Ba-do - di-o - di see their pri-vate yachts gleam. ___ Ba-do di-o-di-o their

life is a dream.) ___ Gee, how luck-y can you, whee, how luck-y can you, wow, how luck-y can you

get? (Ba do - di-o - di they're the luck-i-est guys; ___ the breaks are pil-in' up in front of their eyes.) ___

Now the par-ty's swing-in' and we're still on our feet. How luck-y can you get?

Dig the songs we're sing-in' and the band's got such a beat. How luck-y can you get? ___ We're

class-y en-ter-tain-ers, here's our gold cred-it card. ___ We've got songs by the score, we've got jokes by the yard. So

if you're in the mar-ket for a bar-rel of laughs, __ we're as sharp __ as Gil - lette.

Gee, how luck - y can you, whee, how luck - y can you, wow, how luck - y can you get?

We'll keep en - ter-tain-ing till they give us the boot. __ When the time comes to scoot, we'll just pick up the loot. 'Cause

that's the way we op-er-ate, my part-ner and I, __ we are nev - er in debt. __

Gee, how luck - y can you, whee, how luck - y can you,

wow, how luck - y can you get? _____

THE ADVENTURES OF HUCK FINN
(Main Title)
from Walt Disney's THE ADVENTURES OF HUCK FINN

Music by BILL CONTI

HYMN TO RED OCTOBER
from the Paramount Motion Picture THE HUNT FOR RED OCTOBER

By BASIL POLEDOURIS

HYMN TO THE FALLEN
from the Paramount and DreamWorks Motion Picture SAVING PRIVATE RYAN

Music by JOHN WILLIAMS

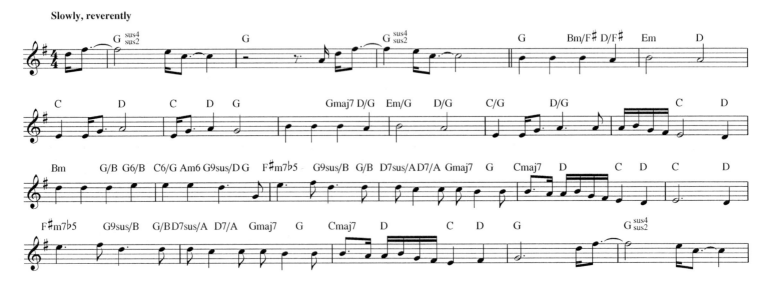

187

I AM A MAN OF CONSTANT SORROW

featured in O BROTHER, WHERE ART THOU?

Words and Music by
CARTER STANLEY

Moderately fast Country

I	am a man	of con - stant
For	six long years	I've been in
It's	fare thee well,	my own true
You	can bur - ry me	in some deep
May -	be your friends think	I'm just a

sor - row.	I've seen trou	- ble all my
trou - ble,	no pleas - ure here	on earth I've
lov - er,	I nev - er ex - pect	to see you a -
val - ley	for man - y years	where I may
stran - ger;	my face you nev	- er will see no

days.	I	bid fare - well
found.	For	in this world
gain,	for	I'm bound to ride
lay,	and	you may learn
more.	But	there is one prom -

— to old Ken - tuck - y,	the place where I
— I'm bound to ram - ble;	I have no friends
— that North - ern rail - road;	per - haps I'll die
— to love an - oth - er	while I am sleep -
— ise that is giv - en:	I'll meet you on

— was born and raised.	The place where he	was born and
— to help me now.	He has no friends	to help him
— up - on this train.	Per - haps he'll die	up - on this
— ing in my grave.	While he is sleep -	ing in his
— God's gold - en shore.	He'll meet you on	God's gold - en

1 - 4   **5**

raised.	shore. *(Instrumental)*
now.	
train.	
grave.	

I BELIEVE I CAN FLY
from SPACE JAM

Words and Music by
ROBERT KELLY

I BELIEVE IN YOU AND ME
from the Touchstone Motion Picture THE PREACHER'S WIFE

Words and Music by DAVID WOLFERT
and SANDY LINZER

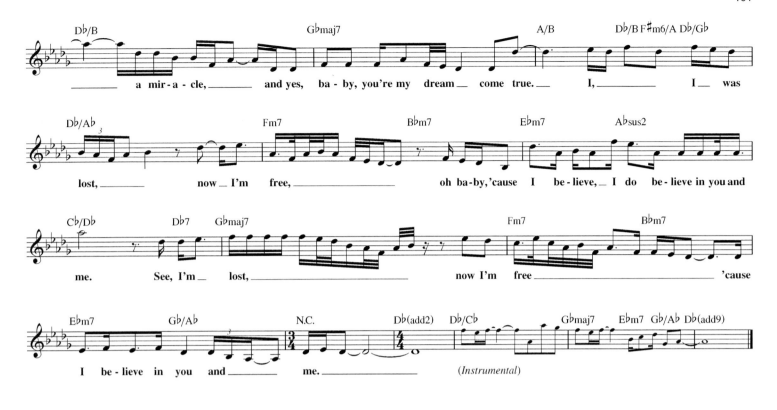

I DON'T WANT TO WALK WITHOUT YOU
from the Paramount Picture SWEATER GIRL

Words by FRANK LOESSER
Music by JULE STYNE

I CONCENTRATE ON YOU
from BROADWAY MELODY OF 1940

Words and Music by
COLE PORTER

I SAY A LITTLE PRAYER

featured in the TriStar Motion Picture MY BEST FRIEND'S WEDDING

Lyric by HAL DAVID
Music by BURT BACHARACH

Moderately

The mo - ment I wake up be - fore __ I put on my make - up __
I run __ for the bus, dear, while rid - ing I think of us, dear. __

__ I say a lit - tle prayer for you. __
__ I say a lit - tle prayer for you. __ While comb - ing my
At work __ I just

hair now and won - d'ring what dress to wear now __ I
take time and all __ through my cof - fee break time __ I

say a lit - tle prayer for you. __ For - ev - er, for - ev - er you'll
say a lit - tle prayer for you. __

stay in my heart __ and I will love you for - ev - er and ev - er. We nev - er will part. __ Oh,

how I'll love you. To - geth - er, to - geth - er, that's how it must be, __ to

live with - out you would on - ly mean heart - break for me. __

My dar - ling, be - lieve me, for me __ there is

no one __ but you. Please __ love me too. __ I'm __ in love with

you. __ An - swer my prayer. Say you love me too.

I FINALLY FOUND SOMEONE
from THE MIRROR HAS TWO FACES

Words and Music by BARBRA STREISAND,
MARVIN HAMLISCH, R.J. LANGE
and BRYAN ADAMS

Moderately slow

Male: I fi-n'lly found some - one who knocks me off my feet. I fi-n'lly found the one _ that

makes me feel com - plete. Female: It start-ed o - ver cof - fee. We start-ed out as friends.

It's fun-ny how from sim-ple things _ the best things be-gin. _ Male: This time it's dif-f'rent.

It's all be-cause of you. _ It's bet-ter than it's ev - er been _ 'cause we can talk it through.

Female: My fa-v'rite line _ was, "Can I call you some - time?" _ It's all you had to say _ to

take my breath a - way. _ Both: This is it. Oh, _ I fi - n'lly found some-one, some-

one to share my life. I fi - n'lly found the one _ to be with ev - 'ry night. 'Cause what- Female:

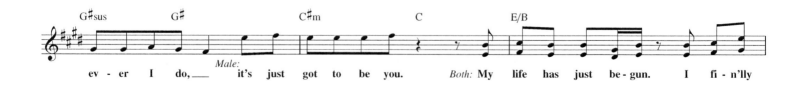

ev - er I do, _ it's just got to be you. Both: My life has just be-gun. I fi-n'lly

I HEAR MUSIC
from the Paramount Picture DANCING ON A DIME

Words by FRANK LOESSER
Music by BURTON LANE

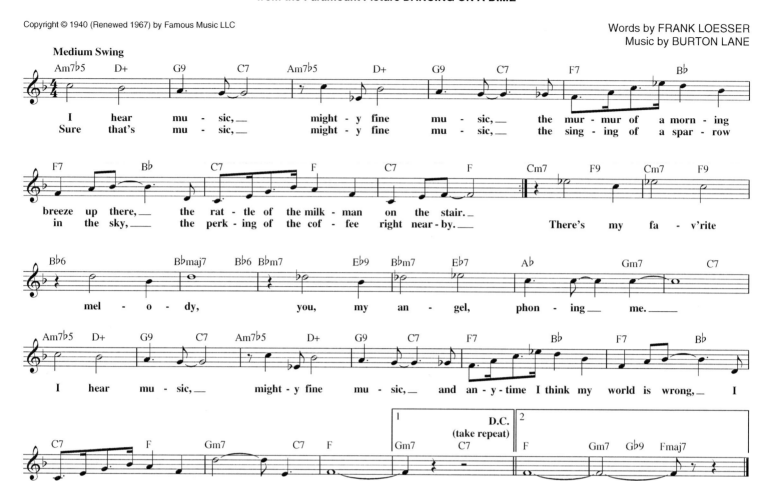

I WALK THE LINE

Words and Music by
JOHN R. CASH

Additional Lyrics

3. As sure as night is dark and day is light,
I keep you on my mind both day and night.
And happiness I've known proves that it's right.
Because you're mine I walk the line.

4. You've got a way to keep me on your side.
You give me cause for love that I can't hide.
For you I know I'd even try to turn the tide.
Because you're mine I walk the line.

5. I keep a close watch on this heart of mine.
I keep my eyes wide open all the time.
I keep the ends out for the tie that binds.
Because you're mine I walk the line.

I WILL REMEMBER YOU

Theme from THE BROTHERS McMULLEN

Words and Music by SARAH McLACHLAN,
SEAMUS EGAN and DAVE MERENDA

I WANT TO SPEND MY LIFETIME LOVING YOU
from the TriStar Motion Picture THE MASK OF ZORRO

Music by JAMES HORNER
Lyric by WILL JENNINGS

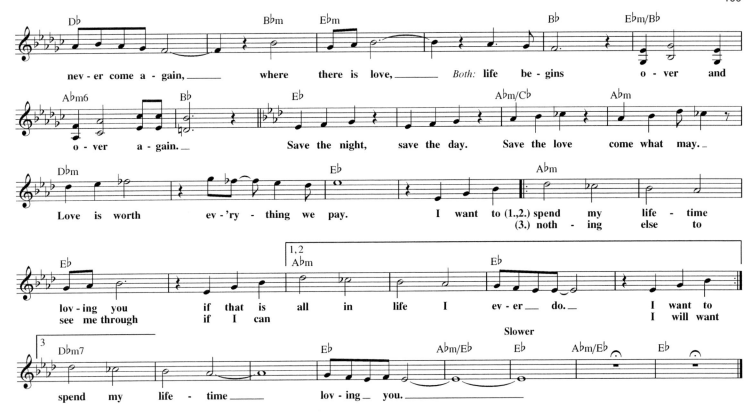

I WILL WAIT FOR YOU
from THE UMBRELLAS OF CHERBOURG

Music by MICHEL LEGRAND
Original French Text by JACQUES DEMY
English Words by NORMAN GIMBEL

I WILL ALWAYS LOVE YOU
from THE BODYGUARD

Words and Music by
DOLLY PARTON

If ___ I ___ should ___ stay, ___ I ___ would ___ on - ly ___ be ___ in ___ your

way. ___ So I'll ___ go, ___ but I ___ know ___ I'll think of

you ev-'ry step of the ___ way. ___ And I ___ will ___ al-ways

love you. ___ I will ___ al-ways love you. ___

You, ___ my dar - ling, you. ___ Hmm. ___ Bit - ter -

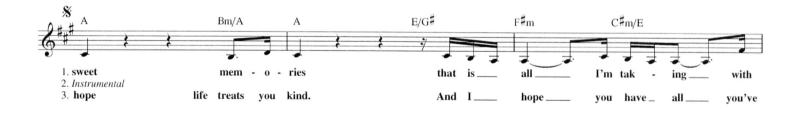

1. sweet ___ mem - o - ries ___ that is ___ all ___ I'm tak - ing ___ with
2. *Instrumental*
3. hope ___ life treats you kind. ___ And I ___ hope ___ you have ___ all ___ you've

me. ___ So, good - bye. ___ Please, ___ don't ___ cry. We both ___
dreamed ___ of ___ And I wish to you ___ joy ___ and hap - pi - ness. But a - bove

know ___ I'm not what you, ___ you need. ___ And I ___ I ___
all this ___ I wish you

I WILL FOLLOW HIM
(I Will Follow You)
featured in the Motion Picture SISTER ACT

English Lyrics by NORMAN GIMBEL and ARTHUR ALTMAN
French Words by JACQUES PLANTE
Music by J.W. STOLE and DEL ROMA

I will fol - low him, fol - low him wher - ev - er he may go. ___ And

near him I al - ways will be, for noth - ing can keep me a - way. He is my des - ti - ny. ___

I will fol - low him. ___ Ev - er since he touched my heart I knew. ___ There

is - n't an o - cean too deep, a moun - tain so high it can keep, keep me a - way, ___

a - way from his love. ___ (Instrumental) I

love him, I love him, I love him. And where he goes I'll fol - low, I'll fol - low, I'll fol - low, I will fol - low

him, ___ fol - low him wher - ev - er he may go. ___ There is - n't an o - cean too

deep, a moun - tain so high it can keep, keep me a - way. I will fol - low

203

him, _____ fol - low him wher - ev - er he may go. _____ There is - n't an o - cean too

deep, a moun - tain so high it can keep, keep me a - way, a - way from his

love. (I love him,) oh, yes, I love ___ him. (I'll fol - low,) I'm gon - na

fol - low. ___ (True love,) he'll al - ways be my true _____ love. (For - ev - er,) from now un - til for -

ev - er. _____ I love him, I love him, I love him. And where he goes I'll fol - low, I'll fol - low, I'll

fol - low. He'll al - ways be my true love, my true love, my true love from now un - til for - ev - er, for - ev - er, for -

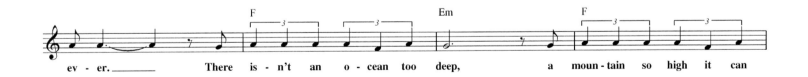

ev - er. _____ There is - n't an o - cean too deep, a moun - tain so high it can

keep, keep me a - way, _____ a - way from his Love. _____

I WILL SURVIVE

featured in THE ADVENTURES OF PRISCILLA, QUEEN OF THE DESERT

Words and Music by DINO FEKARIS
and FREDERICK J. PERREN

Rubato

Am / Dm / G

At first I was a-fraid, I was pet-ri-fied,_ kept think-in' I could nev-er live _ with-out you

Cmaj7 / Fmaj7 / Bm7♭5

by my side. But then I spent so man-y nights _ think-in' how you did me wrong, and I grew

Esus / E **Moderate Dance tempo** Am / Dm

strong, and I learned how to get a-long, _ and so you're back from out-er space; _ I just walked

me, some-bod-y new, _____ I'm not that

G / Cmaj7

in to find _ you here _ with that _ sad look up-on _ your face. I should have changed _

chained-up lit - tle per - son still _ in love with you. _ And so you feel _

Fmaj7 / Bm7♭5

that stu-pid lock, _ I should have made _ you leave your key _ if I'd-ve known _

like drop-pin' in _ and you ex-pect _ me to be free. _ Now I'm sav-

Esus / E / Am

for just _ one sec-ond you'd be back to both-er me. _

-in' all _ my lov-in' for some-one who's lov-in' me. _ Go on now go, walk out the door!

Dm / G / Cmaj7

Just turn a-round _ now, ('cause) you're not wel-come an-y-more.

Fmaj7 / Bm7♭5 / Esus

Weren't you the one _ who tried to hurt _ me with good-bye? _ Did I crum-ble? _ Did you think I'd

E / Am / Dm

lay down _ and die? Oh no, not I. I will sur-vive. _____ Oh _ as

G / Cmaj7 / Fmaj7

long as I know how to love _ I know I'll stay a-live; I've got all my life to live, _ I've got

Bm7♭5 / Esus **To Coda** E

all my love to give _ and I'll sur-vive, I will sur-vive. _____ Hey hey.

all the strength I had not to fall a-part; kept try-in'
hard to mend the piec-es of my bro-ken heart. And I spent, oh, so man-y nights just feel-in'
sor-ry for my-self. I used to cry, but now I *Instrumental ends* It took
hold my head up high and you see
I'll sur-vive.

I WISH I DIDN'T LOVE YOU SO
from the Paramount Picture THE PERILS OF PAULINE

Words and Music by
FRANK LOESSER

I wish I did-n't love you so, my love for you
should have fad-ed long a-go. I
wish I did-n't need your
kiss. Why must your kiss tor-ture me as long as this? I might be
smil-ing by now with some new ten-der friend, smil-ing by now
with my heart on the mend. But when I try, something in that heart says
"No," you're still there. I wish I did-n't love you so.

I'M A BELIEVER
from the DreamWorks Motion Picture SHREK

Words and Music by
NEIL DIAMOND

I'M LATE
from Walt Disney's ALICE IN WONDERLAND

Words by BOB HILLIARD
Music by SAMMY FAIN

I'M OLD FASHIONED
from YOU WERE NEVER LOVELIER

Words by JOHNNY MERCER
Music by JEROME KERN

I'M EASY
from NASHVILLE

Words and Music by
KEITH CARRADINE

I WON'T DANCE
from ROBERTA

Words and Music by JIMMY McHUGH,
DOROTHY FIELDS, JEROME KERN,
OSCAR HAMMERSTEIN II and OTTO HARBACH

I'M PUTTING ALL MY EGGS IN ONE BASKET
from the Motion Picture FOLLOW THE FLEET

Words and Music by
IRVING BERLIN

I'VE GOT YOU UNDER MY SKIN
from BORN TO DANCE

Words and Music by
COLE PORTER

I've got you _____ un-der my skin, _____ I've got you _____ deep in the

heart of me, _____ so deep in my heart, _____ you're real-ly a part of me. _____ I've got you _____

_____ un-der my skin. _____ I tried so _____ not to give in, _____ I

said to my-self, "This af-fair nev-er will go so well." _____ But why should I try to re-

sist when, dar-ling, I know so well _____ I've got you _____ un-der my

skin. _____ I'd sac-ri-fice an-y-thing, come what might, for the sake of hav-ing you near, in spite of a

warn-ing voice that comes in the night and re-peats and re-peats in my ear: _____ "Don't you know, lit-tle fool, _____

_____ you nev-er can win, _____ use your men-tal-i-ty, _____ wake up to re-

al-i-ty." _____ But each time I do, just the thought of you makes me stop, be-fore I be-

gin, 'cause I've got you _____ un-der my skin. _____ I've skin.

I'M STILL HERE
from FOLLIES
featured in the Motion Picture POSTCARDS FROM THE EDGE

Music and Lyrics by
STEPHEN SONDHEIM

I'VE GOT MY LOVE TO KEEP ME WARM
from the 20th Century Fox Motion Picture ON THE AVENUE

Words and Music by
IRVING BERLIN

I'VE HEARD THAT SONG BEFORE
from the Motion Picture YOUTH ON PARADE

Lyric by SAMMY CAHN
Music by JULE STYNE

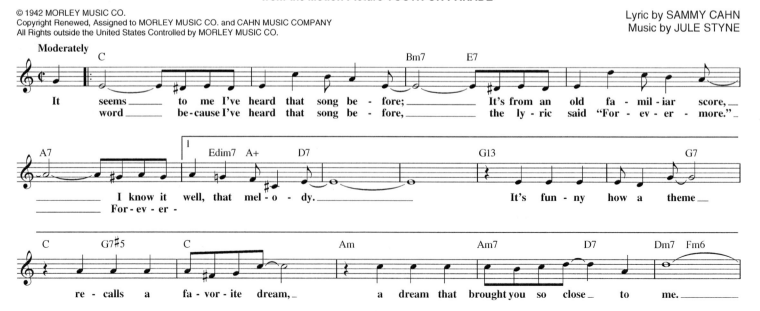

IF I HAD A TALKING PICTURE OF YOU
from SUNNY SIDE UP

Words and Music by RAY HENDERSON,
LEW BROWN and B.G. DeSYLVA

IF I HAD WORDS
featured in the Universal Motion Picture BABE

By JOHN HODGE

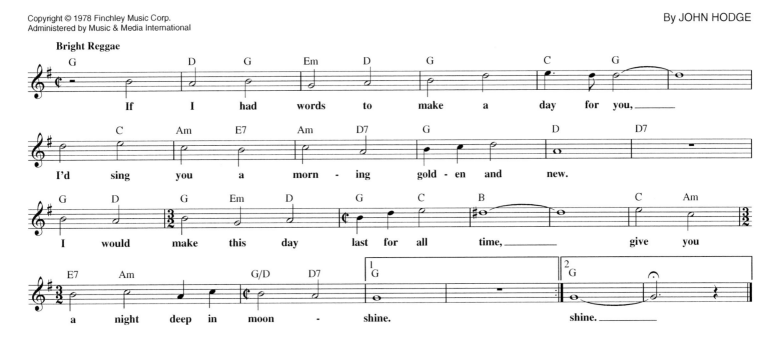

IF I NEVER KNEW YOU
(Love Theme from POCAHONTAS)
from Walt Disney's POCAHONTAS

Music by ALAN MENKEN
Lyrics by STEPHEN SCHWARTZ

IF I WERE A RICH MAN
from the Musical FIDDLER ON THE ROOF

Words by SHELDON HARNICK
Music by JERRY BOCK

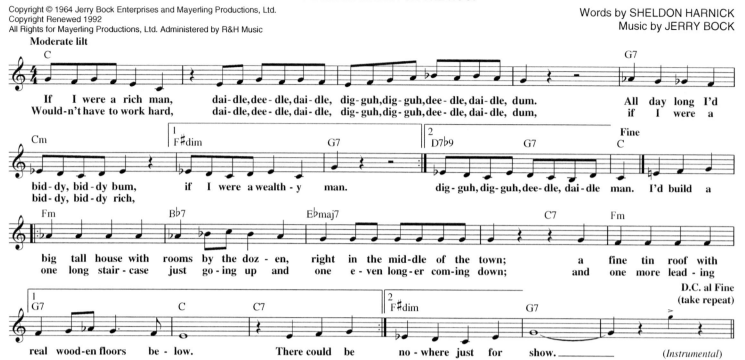

IF MY FRIENDS COULD SEE ME NOW!
from SWEET CHARITY

Music by CY COLEMAN
Words by DOROTHY FIELDS

IF WE HOLD ON TOGETHER

from THE LAND BEFORE TIME

Words and Music by JAMES HORNER
and WILL JENNINGS

Flowingly

Don't lose your way with each pass-ing day. You've come so far, don't throw it a-way.
Souls in the wind must learn how to bend, seek out a star, hold on to the end.

Live be-liev-ing dreams are for weav-ing, won-ders are wait-ing to start.
Val-ley, moun-tain, there is a foun-tain wash-es our tears all a-way.

Live your sto-ry, faith, hope and glo-ry. Hold to the truth in your ____ heart.
Waves are sway-ing, some-one is pray-ing, please let us come home to stay.

If we hold on ____ to-geth ___ er, I know our dreams will nev-er die. ___

Dreams see us through to for-ev ___ er where clouds roll ____ by for

you and ____ I. I. When we are out there in the dark ___ we'll

dream a-bout the sun. ___ In the dark we'll feel the light, ___

warm our hearts ___ ev-'ry-one. ____ If we hold on ____ to-geth ___ er ___

I know our ___ dreams will nev-er die. ___ Dreams see us through to for-ev ___ er as

high as souls can fly, the clouds roll by for you and I. ___

IF YOU LEAVE
from PRETTY IN PINK

Words and Music by PAUL HUMPHREYS,
ANDY McCLUSKEY and MARTIN COOPER

CODA

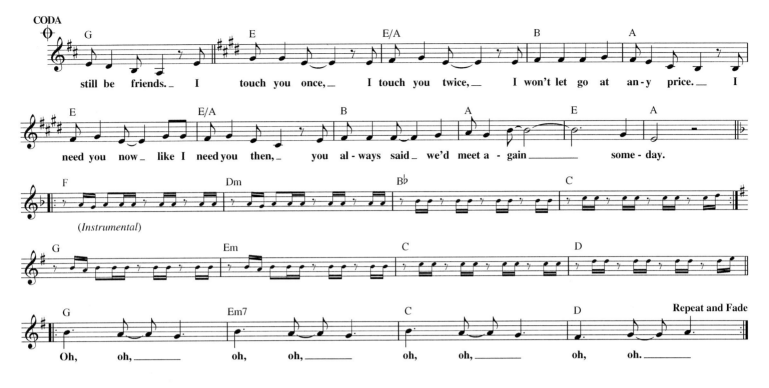

still be friends._ I touch you once,_ I touch you twice,_ I won't let go at an-y price._ I

need you now_ like I need you then,_ you al-ways said_ we'd meet a-gain _____ some-day.

(Instrumental)

Oh,   oh, _____   oh,   oh, _____   oh,   oh, _____   oh,   oh. _____

Repeat and Fade

IL POSTINO
(The Postman)
from IL POSTINO

Music by LUIS BACALOV

Slowly

IF YOU REMEMBER ME
from THE CHAMP

Words by CAROLE BAYER SAGER
Music by MARVIN HAMLISCH

IN THE COOL, COOL, COOL OF THE EVENING
from the Paramount Picture HERE COMES THE GROOM

Words by JOHNNY MERCER
Music by HOAGY CARMICHAEL

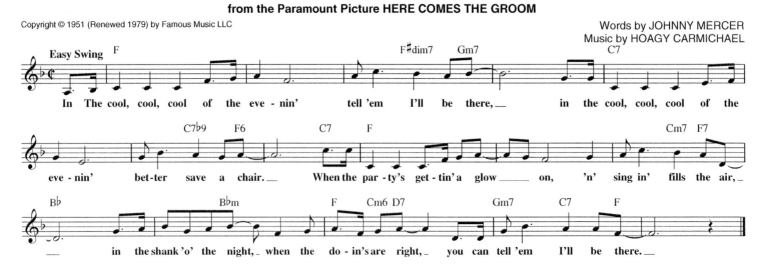

IN THE STILL OF THE NIGHT
from NIGHT AND DAY

Words and Music by
COLE PORTER

Moderately

In the still of the night, _____ as I gaze from my win - dow,

at the moon in its flight, my thoughts all stray to you. _____

In the still of the night, _____ while the world is in slum - ber,

oh, the times with - out num - ber, dar - ling, when I say to you: _____

_____ "Do _____ you love me as I love

you? _____ Are you my life - to - be, my dream come

true?" _____ Or will this dream of mine fade _____ out of

sight _____ like the moon, _____ grow - ing dim, _____ on the rim _____ of the

hill _____ in the chill, _____ still _____ of the night?

1.

_____ night? _____

2.

INNAMORATA
(Sweetheart)
from the Paramount Picture ARTISTS AND MODELS

Words by JACK BROOKS
Music by HARRY WARREN

ISN'T IT ROMANTIC?
from the Paramount Picture LOVE ME TONIGHT

Words by LORENZ HART
Music by RICHARD RODGERS

IRIS

from the Motion Picture CITY OF ANGELS

Words and Music by
JOHN RZEZNIK

With a steady pulse

And I'd give up for-ev-er to touch __ you 'cause I __ know __ that you feel __
__ I could taste __ is this mo - ment, and __ all __ I can breathe
__ fight the tears that ain't com - ing, or the __ mo - ment of truth __

me some - how. You're the clos - est to heav - en that I'll __ ev - er __ be
is your __ life. And soon - er or lat - er it's o - ver.
in your __ lies. When ev - 'ry - thing feels like the mov - ies,

and I __ don't __ wan - na go __ home right now. And all __
I just __ don't __ wan - na miss __ you to -
yeah, you bleed __ just to know __ you're a -

night.
live.

To Coda
And I __ don't want the world __ to see me 'cause I __ don't __ think that they'd __

un - der - stand. When ev - 'ry - thing's __ made to be __ bro - ken

I just __ want __ you to know __ who I __ am. *(Instrumental)*

D.S. al Coda
(take 3rd ending)

And you can't __

CODA
don't want the world __ to see __ me 'cause I __ don't __ think that they'd __ un - der - stand.

When ev - ry - thing's __ made to be __ bro - ken, I just __ want __ you to know __ who I __

am. __ And I __ am. I just __ want __ you to know __ who I __

am. __ I just __ want __ am. ___ *Instrumental solo*
(Vocal 1st time only)

Repeat and Fade

IS YOU IS, OR IS YOU AIN'T
(Ma' Baby)
from FOLLOW THE BOYS

Words and Music by BILLY AUSTIN
and LOUIS JORDAN

ISN'T THIS A LOVELY DAY (TO BE CAUGHT IN THE RAIN?)
from the RKO Radio Motion Picture TOP HAT

Words and Music by
IRVING BERLIN

IT COULD HAPPEN TO YOU
from the Paramount Picture AND THE ANGELS SING

Words by JOHNNY BURKE
Music by JAMES VAN HEUSEN

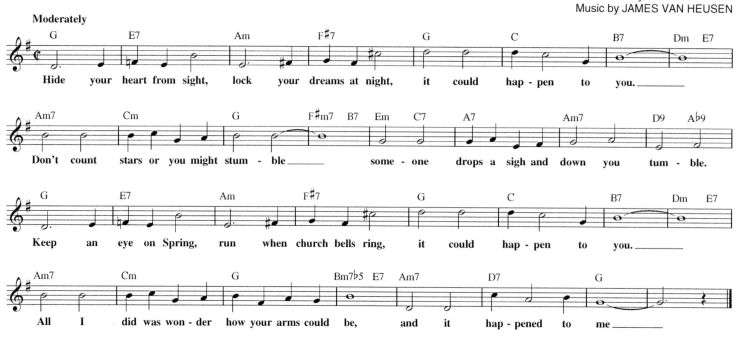

IT MIGHT AS WELL BE SPRING
from STATE FAIR

Lyrics by OSCAR HAMMERSTEIN II
Music by RICHARD RODGERS

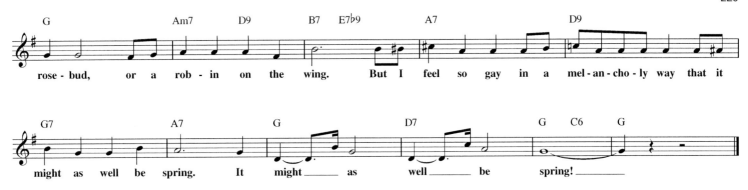

IT ONLY HAPPENS WHEN I DANCE WITH YOU
from the Motion Picture Irving Berlin's EASTER PARADE

Words and Music by
IRVING BERLIN

IT MUST HAVE BEEN LOVE
featured in the Motion Picture PRETTY WOMAN

Words and Music by
PER GESSLE

IT WAS WRITTEN IN THE STARS
from the Motion Picture CASBAH

Lyric by LEO ROBIN
Music by HAROLD ARLEN

IT'S A BIG WIDE WONDERFUL WORLD

By JOHN ROX

IT'S A GRAND NIGHT FOR SINGING
from STATE FAIR

Lyrics by OSCAR HAMMERSTEIN II
Music by RICHARD RODGERS

IT'S A MOST UNUSUAL DAY

from A DATE WITH JUDY

Words by HAROLD ADAMSON
Music by JIMMY McHUGH

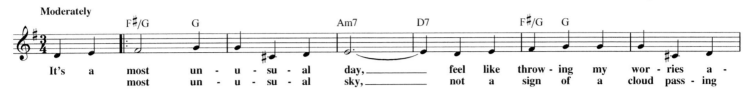

It's a most un-u-su-al day,_____ feel like throw-ing my wor-ries a-
most un-u-su-al sky,_____ not a sign of a cloud pass-ing

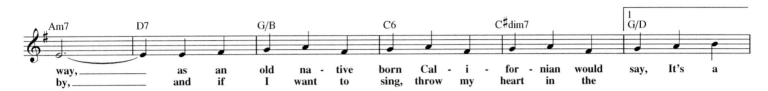

way,_____ as an old na-tive born Cal-i-for-nian would say, It's a
by,_____ and if I want to sing, throw my heart in the

most un-u-su-al day._____ There's a ring. It's a most un-u-su-al

day._____ There are peo-ple meet-ing peo-ple,_____ there is sun-shine_____

_____ ev-'ry-where._____ There are peo-ple greet-ing peo-ple_____ and a

feel-ing of spring in the air._____ It's a most un-u-su-al time._____

_____ I keep feel-ing my tem-p'ra-ture climb._____ If my heart won't be-have in the

u-su-al way, well there's on-ly one thing to say,_____ it's a most un-

u-su-al, most un-u-su-al, most un-u-su-al day._____

234

IT'S A NEW WORLD
from the Motion Picture A STAR IS BORN

Lyric by IRA GERSHWIN
Music by HAROLD ARLEN

IT'S MY TURN
from IT'S MY TURN

Words and Music by CAROLE BAYER SAGER
and MICHAEL MASSER

IT'S EASY TO REMEMBER
from the Paramount Picture MISSISSIPPI

Words by LORENZ HART
Music by RICHARD RODGERS

Your sweet ex - pres - sion,_____ the smile you gave me,_____ the way you looked when we
whis - per:_____ "I'll al - ways love you,"_____ I know it's o - ver and

met, }
yet, }   it's eas - y to re - mem - ber but so hard to for -

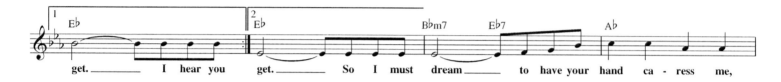

get._____ I hear you get._____ So I must dream_____ to have your hand ca - ress me,

fin - gers press me tight._____ I'd rath - er dream_____ than have that lone - ly feel - ing

steal - ing through the night._____ Each lit - tle mo - ment_____ is clear be - fore me,_____ and though it

brings me re - gret, it's eas - y to re - mem - ber, and so hard to for - get.

IT'S ONLY A PAPER MOON
featured in the Motion Picture TAKE A CHANCE

Lyric by BILLY ROSE and E.Y. "Yip" HARBURG
Music by HAROLD ARLEN

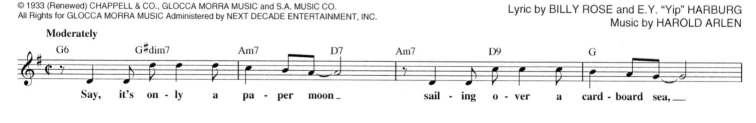

Say, it's on - ly a pa - per moon___ sail - ing o - ver a card - board sea,___

but it would - n't be make - be - lieve___ if you___ be - lieved___ in me.

Yes, it's on-ly a can-vas sky ___ hang-ing o-ver a mus-lin tree, ___ but it wouldn't be make-be-lieve, ___ if you ___ be-lieved ___ in me. ___ With-out your love, it's a hon-ky-tonk pa-rade. With-out your love, it's a mel-o-dy played in a pen-ny ar-cade. It's a Bar-num and Bai-ley world, ___ just as phon-y as it can be, ___ but it would-n't be make-be-lieve ___ if you ___ be-lieved ___ in me. ___

THEME FROM "JAWS"
from the Universal Picture JAWS

By JOHN WILLIAMS

JESSICA'S THEME
(Breaking In The Colt)
from THE MAN FROM SNOWY RIVER

By BRUCE ROWLAND

JINGLE JANGLE JINGLE
(I Got Spurs)
from the Paramount Picture THE FOREST RANGERS

Words by FRANK LOESSER
Music by JOSEPH J. LILLEY

I got spurs that Jin - gle Jan - gle Jin - gle, _____ as I go rid - in' mer - ri - ly a -
sing, "Oh, ain't you glad you're sin - gle!" _____ and that song ain't so ver - y far from

long. _____ And they
wrong. _____ ___ Oh, Lil - lie Belle, _____ oh, Lil - lie Belle, _____ though I may have done some

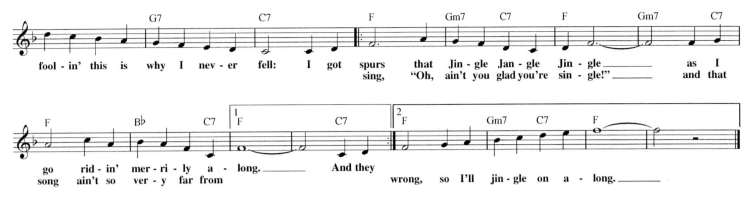

JIVE TALKIN'
from SATURDAY NIGHT FEVER

Words and Music by BARRY GIBB,
ROBIN GIBB and MAURICE GIBB

THE JOHN DUNBAR THEME
from DANCES WITH WOLVES

By JOHN BARRY

THEME FROM "JURASSIC PARK"
from the Universal Motion Picture JURASSIC PARK

Composed by JOHN WILLIAMS

KISSIN' COUSINS
from KISSIN' COUSINS

Words and Music by FRED WISE
and RANDY STARR

JOURNEY TO THE PAST
from the Twentieth Century Fox Motion Picture ANASTASIA

Words and Music by LYNN AHRENS
and STEPHEN FLAHERTY

KING OF WISHFUL THINKING
from the Motion Picture PRETTY WOMAN

Words and Music by MARTIN PAGE,
PETER COX and RICHARD DRUMMIE

KISS THE GIRL
from Walt Disney's THE LITTLE MERMAID

Lyrics by HOWARD ASHMAN
Music by ALAN MENKEN

KOKOMO
from the Motion Picture COCKTAIL

Words and Music by MIKE LOVE,
TERRY MELCHER, JOHN PHILLIPS
and SCOTT McKENZIE

Moderately bright

A - ru - ba, Ja - mai - ca, oo ___ I wan - na take ya. Ber - mu - da, Ba - ha - ma, come ___ on, pret - ty ma - ma. Key

Lar - go, Mon - te - go, ba - by, why don't we we go, Ja - mai - ca. Off the Flor - i - da Keys ___ We'll put out to sea

___ there's a place called Ko - ko - mo. ___ That's where we want to go ___ to get a -
___ we'll per - fect our chem - is - try. ___ By and by we'll de - fy ___ a lit - tle bit of

way from it all. ___ Bod - ies in the sand, ___ trop - i - cal drink melt - ing
grav - i - ty. Af - ter - noon de - light, ___ cock - tails and

in your hand. ___ We'll be fall - ing in love ___ to the rhy - thm of a steel - drum band ___
moon - lit nights. ___ the dream - y look in your eye, ___ give me a trop - i - cal con - tact high

A - ru - ba,
down in Ko - ko - mo ___ } Ja - mai - ca, oo ___ I wan - na take you to Ber - mu - da, Ba - ha - ma. Come
way down in Ko - ko - mo ___ }

Oo ___ I wan - na take you down to
___ on pret - ty ma - ma. Key Lar - go, Mon - te - go, ba - by, why don't we go. Ko - ko - mo. ___ We'll

get there fast ___ and then we'll take it slow. ___ That's where ___ we ___ wan - na go, ___

way down in Ko - ko - mo. ___
(Mar - tin - ique, that Montser - rat mys - tique.)
(Port Au Prince, I wan - na catch a glimpse.)
(Instrumental)

Ev - 'ry - bod - y knows ___ a lit - tle place like Ko - ko - mo. ___

Now if you wan-na go___ to get a-way from it all,___ go down to Ko-ko-mo.

ru-ba, Ja-mai-ca, oo___ I wan-na take ya to Ber-mu-da, Ba-ha-ma. Come___ on, pret-ty ma-ma. Key

Lar-go, Mon-te-go, ba - by, why don't we go. Ko-ko-mo.___ We'll get there fast___ and then we'll

take it slow.___ That's where we___ wan-na go,___ way down in Ko-ko-mo.

LA DOLCE VITA
Theme from the Film LA DOLCE VITA

Music by NINO ROTA
Lyrics by DINO VERDE

KYRIE FOR THE MAGDALENE
from THE DA VINCI CODE

By RICHARD HARVEY

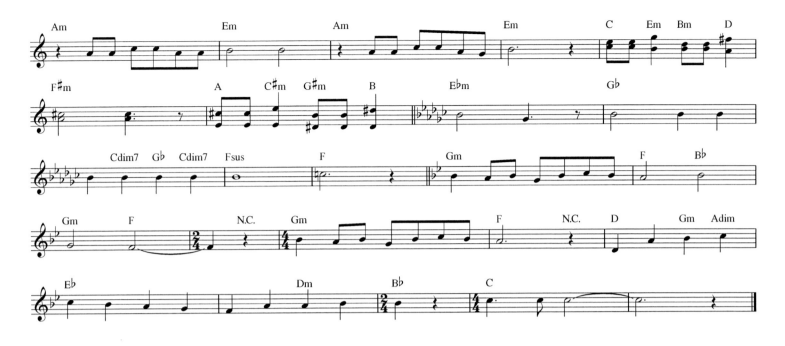

LA PASSERELLA DI ADDIO
Theme from the Film 8 1/2

Music by NINO ROTA

THE LADY'S IN LOVE WITH YOU
from the Paramount Picture SOME LIKE IT HOT

Words by FRANK LOESSER
Music by BURTON LANE

THEME FROM "LASSIE"
from the Paramount Motion Picture LASSIE

Music by BASIL POLEDOURIS

LAST DANCE
from THANK GOD IT'S FRIDAY

Words and Music by
PAUL JABARA

THE LAST TIME I FELT LIKE THIS
from SAME TIME, NEXT YEAR

Words by ALAN BERGMAN and MARILYN BERGMAN
Music by MARVIN HAMLISCH

Moderately

Hel - lo, I don't _ e - ven know _ your _ name, but I'm hop - in' all _ the
lo, I can't _ wait till we're _ a - lone, some - where qui - et on _ our

same this is more than just a sim - ple hel - lo. Hel - lo, do I smile and walk _ a -
own so that we can fall the rest of the way. I know that be - fore the night _ is

way? No, I think I'll smile _ and stay to see where this might go.)
thru, I'll be talk - ing love _ to you, mean - ing ev - 'ry word I _ say.) 'Cause the last time I felt like this

I was fall - ing in love, fall - ing and feel - ing _ I'd nev - er fall in love a - gain. Yes, the

last time I felt like this was long be - fore I knew _ what I'm feel - ing now with

you. _____ Hel - feel - ing now with you. Oh, the last time I felt like this

I was fall - ing in love, fall - ing and feel - ing _ I'd nev - er fall in love a - gain. Yes, the

Repeat and Fade

last time I felt like this was long be - fore I knew _ what I'm feel - ing now with you. Oh, the

THE LAST TIME I SAW PARIS
from LADY, BE GOOD
from TILL THE CLOUDS ROLL BY

Lyrics by OSCAR HAMMERSTEIN II
Music by JEROME KERN

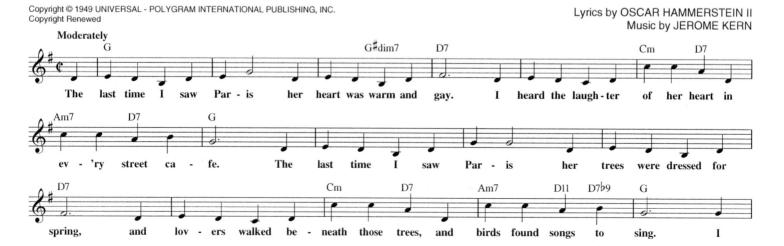

Moderately

The last time I saw Par - is her heart was warm and gay. I heard the laugh - ter of her heart in

ev - 'ry street ca - fe. The last time I saw Par - is her trees were dressed for

spring, and lov - ers walked be - neath those trees, and birds found songs to sing. I

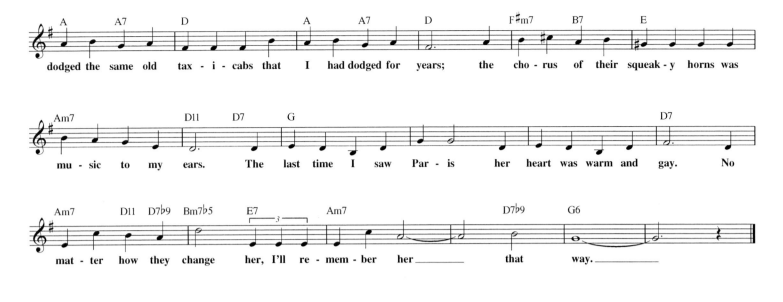

dodged the same old tax - i - cabs that I had dodged for years; the cho - rus of their squeak - y horns was

mu - sic to my ears. The last time I saw Par - is her heart was warm and gay. No

mat - ter how they change her, I'll re - mem - ber her _____ that way. _____

THEME FROM "LAWRENCE OF ARABIA"
from LAWRENCE OF ARABIA

By MAURICE JARRE

Slowly, with expression

LEARN TO BE LONELY
from THE PHANTOM OF THE OPERA

Music by ANDREW LLOYD WEBBER
Lyrics by CHARLES HART

LET YOURSELF GO

from the Motion Picture FOLLOW THE FLEET
from SPEEDWAY

Words and Music by
IRVING BERLIN

LET THE RIVER RUN
Theme from the Motion Picture WORKING GIRL

Words and Music by
CARLY SIMON

Slowly, freely

Let the riv-er run, let all the dream-ers wake the na-tion. Come,___ the new Je-

Moderately

ru-sa-lem. Sil-ver cit-ies rise; the morn-ing lights the streets that

lead them. And si-rens call them on with a song. It's ask-ing for the

tak-ing, trem-bling, sha-ak-ing.___ Oh,___ my heart is ach-ing. We're

com-ing to the edge, run-ning on the wa-ter, com-ing through the fog, your sons and daugh-ters.

We,___ the great and small,___ stand on a star and blaze a trail___ of de-sire through the

(D.S.) Instrumental solo

To Coda

dar-kling___ dawn. Solo ends It's ask-ing for the tak-ing. Come

run with me now; the sky is the col-or of blue you've nev-er e-ven seen in the eyes of your lov-er.

D.S. al Coda

ach-ing. We're com-ing to the edge, run-ning on the wa-ter, com-ing through the fog, your sons and daugh-ters.

LEGENDS OF THE FALL
from TriStar Pictures' LEGENDS OF THE FALL

Composed by JAMES HORNER

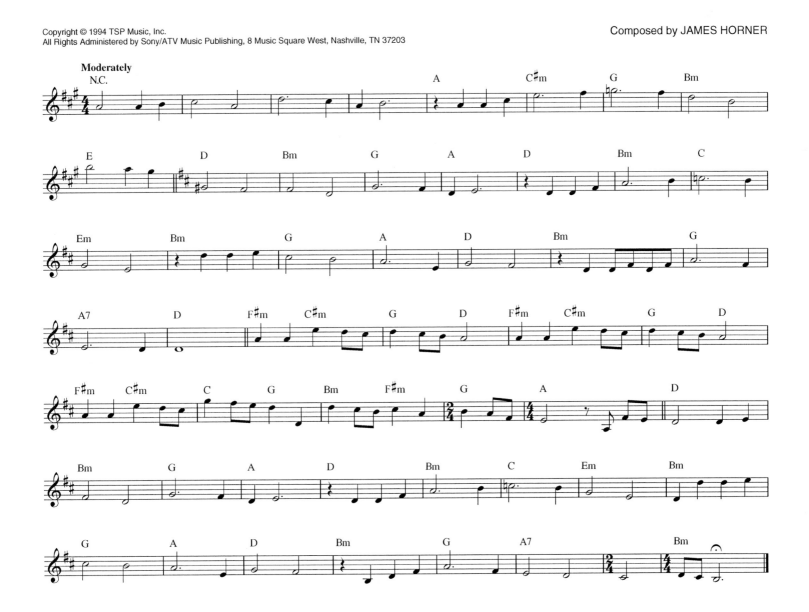

LET'S FACE THE MUSIC AND DANCE
from the Motion Picture FOLLOW THE FLEET

Words and Music by
IRVING BERLIN

LET'S GO FLY A KITE
from Walt Disney's MARY POPPINS

Words and Music by RICHARD M. SHERMAN
and ROBERT B. SHERMAN

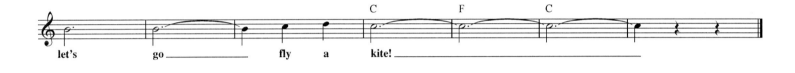

With gusto

Let's go fly a kite up to the high-est height! Let's go fly a kite and send it soar-ing up through the at-mos-phere, up where the air is clear. Oh, let's go _____ fly a kite! _____

LONG AGO
(And Far Away)
from COVER GIRL

Words by IRA GERSHWIN
Music by JEROME KERN

Moderately slow

Long a-go and far a-way, I dreamed a dream one day, and now that dream is here be-side me.

Chills run up and down my spine. A-lad-din's lamp is mine. The dream I dreamed was not de-nied me.

Long the skies were o-ver-cast, but now the clouds have passed; you're here at last! _____ Just one look and then I knew _____ that all I longed for long a-go was you. _____

LET'S GO CRAZY

Words and Music by
PRINCE

(Spoken:) *Dearly beloved, we r gathered here today   2 get through this thing called life.   Electric word, "life"; it means forever, and*

that's a mightly long time. But I'm here 2   tell u there's something else: the afterworld, a world   of never-ending happiness;   u can

always see the sun, day or night.   So when u call up that shrink in Beverly Hills, u know the one,   Dr. Everything'll be alright,

instead of asking him how much of your time   is left, ask him how much of your mind, baby. 'cuz   in this life things r much harder than in the

afterworld.   In this life you're on your own.

And if de el - e - va - tor tries 2 bring __ u down,   go cra - zy; __

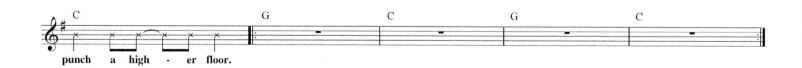

punch   a high - er floor.

If u don't like   the world you're liv - in' in,
all ex - cit - ed,   but we don't know why.

take a look a - round   u;   at least u got friends.   U see, I
May - be it's 'cuz   we're all gon - na die.   And

LET'S HEAR IT FOR THE BOY
from the Paramount Motion Picture FOOTLOOSE

Words by DEAN PITCHFORD
Music by TOM SNOW

Moderately bright

1. My ba - by, he don't talk sweet; _ he ain't got much to say. _____ But he
2. (See additional lyrics)

loves me, loves me, loves _ me; I know that he loves me an - y - way. And

may - be he don't dress fine, _ but I don't real - ly mind. _____ 'Cause

ev - 'ry time _ he pulls me near ⎱ I just wan - na cheer; _ let's hear it for _ the boy, _
Ev - 'ry time _ he pulls me near ⎰

let's give the boy _ a hand, _____ let's hear it for _ my ba - by, _____

you know you got - ta un - der - stand. _____ Oh, _____ may be he's _ no Ro - me - o, _____ but

he's my lov - in' one - man show. Oh whoa, whoa, whoa, let's hear it for the boy. _

To Coda ⊕

1.

2. My _____ **D.S. al Coda**

CODA

whoa, let's hear it for _ the boy, _

Repeat ad lib. and Fade

(Bkgd.) Let's hear it for the boy. _ Let's hear it for my man. _ Let's hear it for _ the boy. _
Let's hear it for my ba - by.

Additional Lyrics

2. My baby may not be rich;
   He's watchin' ev'ry dime.
   But he loves me, loves me, loves me.
   We always have a real good time.
   And maybe he sings off key,
   But that's all right by me, yeah.
   But what he does, he does so well.
   Makes me wanna yell.
   Chorus

LOOKIN' FOR LOVE
from URBAN COWBOY

Words and Music by WANDA MALLETTE,
PATTI RYAN and BOB MORRISON

THE LOOK OF LOVE
from CASINO ROYALE

Words by HAL DAVID
Music by BURT BACHARACH

LOUIE, LOUIE
featured in the Motion Picture ANIMAL HOUSE

Words and Music by
RICHARD BERRY

LOVE IS ALL AROUND

featured on the Motion Picture Soundtrack FOUR WEDDINGS AND A FUNERAL

Words and Music by
REG PRESLEY

Additional Lyrics

2. I see your face before me
   As I lay on my bed;
   I cannot get to thinking
   Of all the things you said.
   You gave your promise to me
   And I gave mine to you;
   I need someone beside me
   In everything I do.
   Chorus

LOUISE
from the Paramount Picture INNOCENTS OF PARIS

Words by LEO ROBIN
Music by RICHARD A. WHITING

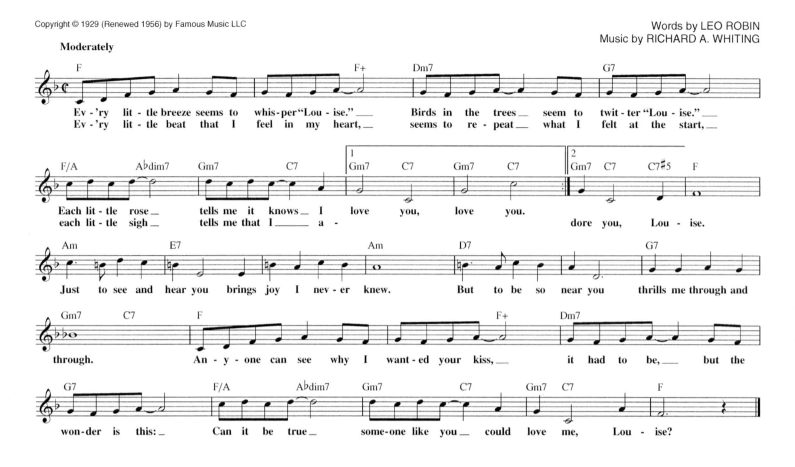

A LOVE BEFORE TIME
from the Motion Picture CROUCHING TIGER, HIDDEN DRAGON

Words and Music by JAMES SCHAMUS,
TAN DUN and JORGE CALANDRELLI

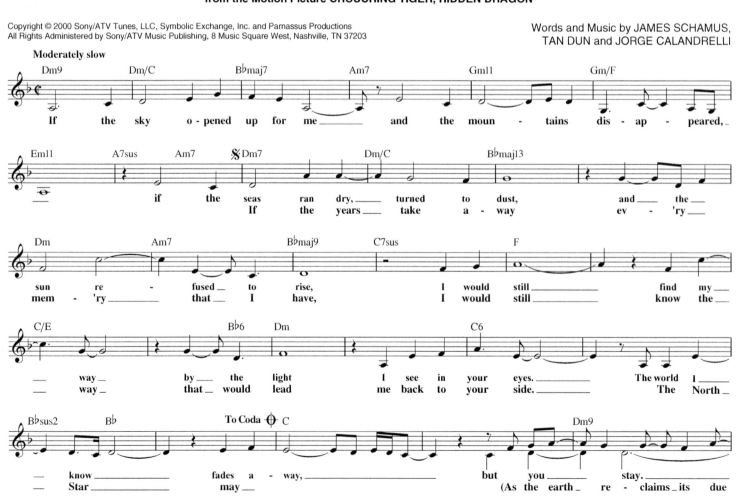

LOVE LETTERS
Theme from the Paramount Picture LOVE LETTERS

Words by EDWARD HEYMAN
Music by VICTOR YOUNG

LOVE ME OR LEAVE ME
from LOVE ME OR LEAVE ME

Lyrics by GUS KAHN
Music by WALTER DONALDSON

LOVE ON THE ROCKS
from the Motion Picture THE JAZZ SINGER

Words and Music by NEIL DIAMOND
and GILBERT BECAUD

LOVE ME TENDER
from LOVE ME TENDER

Words and Music by ELVIS PRESLEY
and VERA MATSON

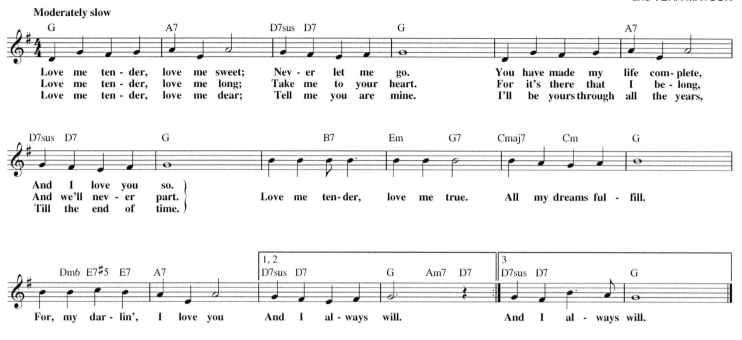

Love me ten-der, love me sweet; Nev-er let me go. You have made my life com-plete,
Love me ten-der, love me long; Take me to your heart. For it's there that I be-long,
Love me ten-der, love me dear; Tell me you are mine. I'll be yours through all the years,

And I love you so.)
And we'll nev-er part.)   Love me ten-der, love me true. All my dreams ful - fill.
Till the end of time.)

For, my dar-lin', I love you And I al - ways will. And I al - ways will.

LOVE THEME
from CINEMA PARADISO

Music by ANDREA MORRICONE

LOVER
from the Paramount Picture LOVE ME TONIGHT

Words by LORENZ HART
Music by RICHARD RODGERS

LOVE, YOU DIDN'T DO RIGHT BY ME

from the Motion Picture Irving Berlin's WHITE CHRISTMAS

Words and Music by
IRVING BERLIN

MAKIN' WHOOPEE!

from WHOOPEE!

Lyrics by GUS KAHN
Music by WALTER DONALDSON

A MAN AND A WOMAN
(Un Homme Et Une Femme)
from A MAN AND A WOMAN

Original Words by PIERRE BAROUH
English Words by JERRY KELLER
Music by FRANCIS LAI

MAKING CHRISTMAS
from Tim Burton's THE NIGHTMARE BEFORE CHRISTMAS

Music and Lyrics by
DANNY ELFMAN

THE MAN FROM SNOWY RIVER
(Main Title Theme)
from THE MAN FROM SNOWY RIVER

By BRUCE ROWLAND

THE MAN THAT GOT AWAY
from the Motion Picture A STAR IS BORN

Lyric by IRA GERSHWIN
Music by HAROLD ARLEN

MANIAC
from the Paramount Picture FLASHDANCE

Words and Music by MICHAEL SEMBELLO
and DENNIS MATKOSKY

MAYBE THIS TIME
from the Musical CABARET

Words by FRED EBB
Music by JOHN KANDER

Slowly

May-be this time _ I'll be luck-y. _ May-be this time he'll stay.
Ev-'ry-bo-dy _ loves a win-ner _ So no-bo-dy _ loved me.

May-be this time, _ For the first time, _ love won't hur-ry a-way.
La-dy Peace-ful, _ La-dy Hap-py, _ That's what I long to be.

He will hold me fast. I'll be home at last.
All the odds are

Not a los-er _ an-y-more, _ like the last time _ and the time be-fore. _

in my fa-vor, _ Some-thing's bound _ to be-gin. It's _ got to hap-pen _

hap-pen some-time, _ May-be this time I'll win. _____

MEET ME IN ST. LOUIS, LOUIS
from MEET ME IN ST. LOUIS

Words by ANDREW B. STERLING
Music by KERRY MILLS

Fast waltz

Meet me in St. Lou-is, Lou-is, meet me at the fair. _____

_ Don't tell me the lights are shin-ing an-y

place but there. _ We will dance the Hooch-ee Kooch-ee,

_ I will be your toots-ie woots-ie; _____ meet me

in St. Lou-is, Lou-is, meet me at the fair. _____

MEMORIES OF YOU
from THE BENNY GOODMAN STORY

Lyric by ANDY RAZAF
Music by EUBIE BLAKE

MEXICALI ROSE
from MEXICALI ROSE

Words by HELEN STONE
Music by JACK B. TENNEY

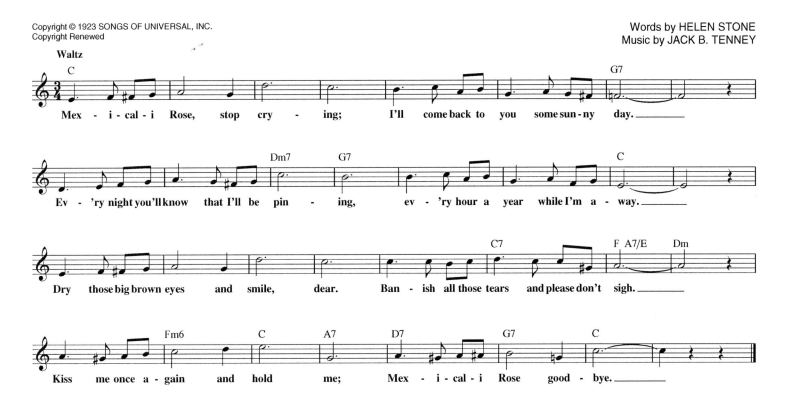

MIDNIGHT COWBOY
from the Motion Picture MIDNIGHT COWBOY

Music by JOHN BARRY
Lyric by JACK GOLD

Moderately slow

(Mid-night cow-boy, mid-night cow-boy, see the lone-some mid-night cow-boy.) Once _____ his hopes were

high as the sky, once _____ a dream was eas-y to buy. _____ Too soon, _____ his ea-ger

fin-gers were burned, soon _____ life's lone-ly les-sons are learned. Hearts _____ are made for car-ing,

life _____ is made for shar - ing. Love _____ is all that's left in the end.

CODA

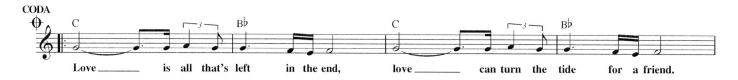

Love _____ is all that's left in the end, love _____ can turn the tide for a friend.

Love _____ can hold a dream to-geth-er, love _____ is all that lasts for-ev-er.

MIMI
from the Paramount Picture LOVE ME TONIGHT

Words by LORENZ HART
Music by RICHARD RODGERS

Cheerfully

Mi-mi, you fun-ny lit-tle good for noth-ing Mi-mi, am I the guy?

_____ Mi-mi, you sun-ny lit-tle hon-ey of a Mi-mi, I'm aim-ing

high! _____ Mi-mi, you've got me sad and dream-y, you could free _____ me, if you'd see _____

_____ me, Mi-mi, you know I'd like to have a lit-tle son of a Mi-mi bye and bye.

MISSION: IMPOSSIBLE THEME
from the Paramount Motion Picture MISSION: IMPOSSIBLE

By LALO SCHIFRIN

MONA LISA
from the Paramount Picture CAPTAIN CAREY, U.S.A.

Words and Music by JAY LIVINGSTON
and RAY EVANS

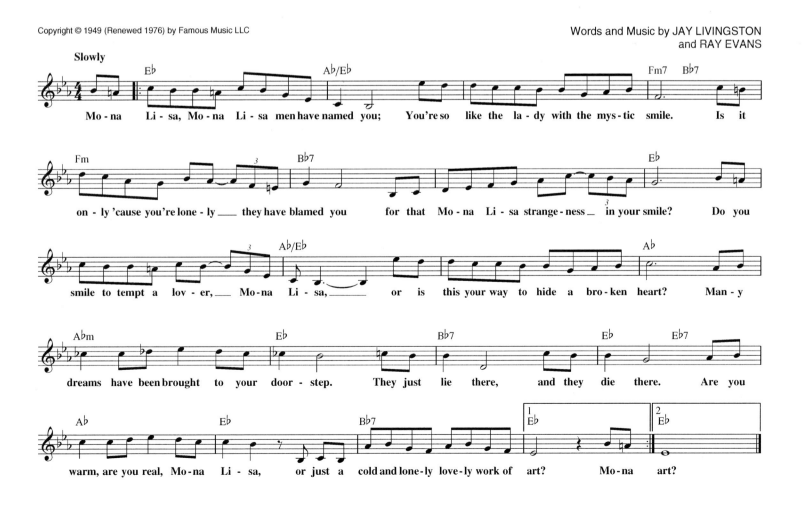

MISS MISERY
from the Miramax Motion Picture GOOD WILL HUNTING

Written by ELLIOTT SMITH

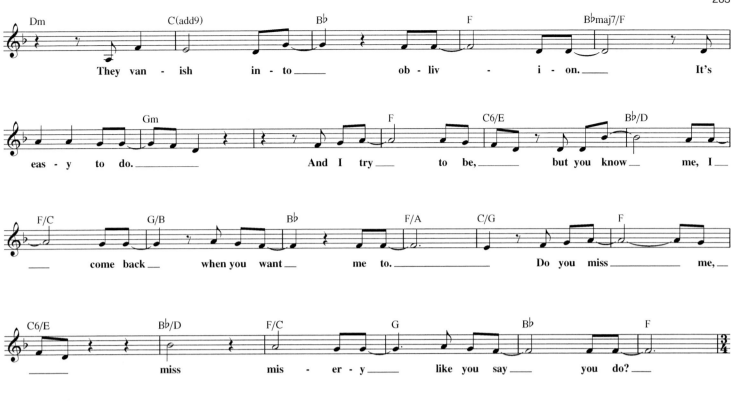

MOON RIVER
from the Paramount Picture BREAKFAST AT TIFFANY'S

Words by JOHNNY MERCER
Music by HENRY MANCINI

MONEY, MONEY
from the Musical CABARET

Words by FRED EBB
Music by JOHN KANDER

Moderately bright

Mon-ey makes the world go a-round, the world go a-round, the world go a-round.

Mon-ey makes the world go a-round, it makes the world go round. *Boy:* A

Girl: A mark, a yen, a buck or a pound

mark, a yen, a buck, or a pound, a buck or a pound, a buck or a pound is

Both: all that makes the world go a-round, that clink-ing, clank-ing sound can make the world go

round. Mon-ey, mon-ey, mon-ey, mon-ey, mon-ey, mon-ey, mon-ey, mon-ey, mon-ey, mon-ey, mon-ey, mon-ey.

Girl: Mon-ey, mon-ey, mon-ey, mon-ey, mon-ey, mon-ey, mon-ey, mon-ey, mon-ey, mon-ey, mon-ey, mon-ey,

Boy: If you hap-pen to be rich, and you feel like a night's en-ter-tain-ment, you can

mon-ey, mon-ey, mon-ey, mon-ey, mon-ey, mon-ey, mon-ey, mon-ey, mon-ey, mon-ey, mon-ey, mon-ey,

pay for a gay es-ca-pade. If you hap-pen to be rich, and a-lone, and you

mon-ey, mon-ey, mon-ey, mon-ey, mon-ey, mon-ey, mon-ey, mon-ey.

need a com-pan-ion, you can ring ting-a-ling for the If you hap-pen to be

Mon-ey, mon-ey, mon-ey, mon-ey, mon-ey, mon-ey, mon-ey, mon-ey, mon-ey, mon-ey, mon-ey, mon-ey,

rich and you find you are left by your lov-er, tho you moan and you groan quite a

Both:

lot, you can take it on the chin, call a cab, and be-gin to re-cov-er on your four-teen car-at

yacht. *Girl:* What? *Both:* Mon-ey makes the world go a-round, the world go a-round, the world go a-round.

MOONLIGHT
from the Paramount Motion Picture SABRINA

Lyric by ALAN and MARILYN BERGMAN
Music by JOHN WILLIAMS

MOONLIGHT BECOMES YOU
from the Paramount Picture ROAD TO MOROCCO

Words by JOHNNY BURKE
Music by JAMES VAN HEUSEN

MORE
(Ti Guarderò Nel Cuore)
from the film MONDO CANE

Music by NINO OLIVIERO and RIZ ORTOLANI
Italian Lyrics by MARCELLO CIORCIOLINI
English Lyrics by NORMAN NEWELL

MRS. ROBINSON
from THE GRADUATE

Words and Music by
PAUL SIMON

most of all,___ you've got to hide___ it from the kids.___ Coo, coo, ca-choo,___
Ev-'ry way you___ look___ at it, ___ you lose.   Where have you gone___

Mrs.___ Rob - in - son, ___ Je - sus loves you more___ than you___ will
Joe Di - Mag - gi - o?___ A   na - tion turns___ its___ lone - ly eyes___ to

know. _____ (Wo, wo, wo.) ___   God bless you, please, Mrs.___ Rob - in - son, ___
you. _____ (Woo, woo, woo.) ___   What's that you say, Mrs.___ Rob - in - son, ___

Heav - en holds a place___ for those___ who pray._____   (Hey, hey, hey,_____
"Jolt - in' Joe"___ has left and gone___ a - way._____   (Hey, hey, hey,_____

___ hey, hey, hey.) _____
___ hey, hey, hey.) _____

MURDER ON THE ORIENT EXPRESS
from the Paramount Motion Picture MURDER ON THE ORIENT EXPRESS

Copyright © 1974 (Renewed 2002) by EMI Film and Theatre Music Ltd.
All Rights in the U.S. Administered by Famous Music LLC

Music by RICHARD RODNEY BENNETT

THE MUSIC OF GOODBYE
Love Theme from OUT OF AFRICA

Music by JOHN BARRY
Words by ALAN and MARILYN BERGMAN

A song I know so well, _____ the mu - sic of good - bye a - gain. _____

_____ It's there each time we say "hel - lo." _____ As al - ways there's no rea - son why a - gain. _____

_____ You kiss me with your eyes _____ and in your arms I fly a - gain. _____ But e - ven as we

touch the clouds, _____ there in the qui - et is good - bye a - gain. _____ Per - haps the way I

hold you _____ makes you a - fraid I'll hold you; _____ makes you a - fraid to love me. _____

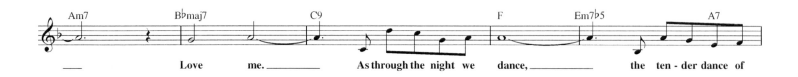

_____ Love me. _____ As through the night we dance, _____ the ten - der dance of

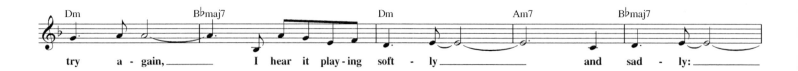

try a - gain, _____ I hear it play - ing soft - ly _____ and sad - ly: _____

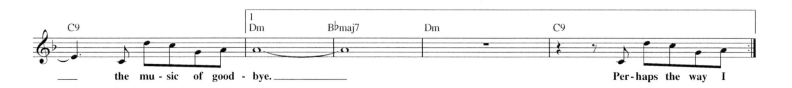

_____ the mu - sic of good - bye. Per - haps the way I

bye. _____ Good - bye. _____ Good - bye.

MY FATHER'S FAVORITE
from SENSE AND SENSIBILITY

By PATRICK DOYLE

MY FUNNY FRIEND AND ME
from Walt Disney Pictures' THE EMPEROR'S NEW GROOVE

Lyrics by STING
Music by STING and DAVID HARTLEY

293

MY HEART WILL GO ON

(Love Theme from 'Titanic')

from the Paramount and Twentieth Century Fox Motion Picture TITANIC

Music by JAMES HORNER
Lyric by WILL JENNINGS

MY OLD FLAME
from the Paramount Picture BELLE OF THE NINETIES

Words and Music by ARTHUR JOHNSTON
and SAM COSLOW

THE NAKED GUN FROM THE FILES OF POLICE SQUAD!

Theme from the Paramount Picture THE NAKED GUN FROM THE FILES OF POLICE SQUAD!
from The Paramount Picture NAKED GUN 33-1/3 (THE FINAL INSULT)

Music by IRA NEWBORN

THE NEARNESS OF YOU
from the Paramount Picture ROMANCE IN THE DARK

Words by NED WASHINGTON
Music by HOAGY CARMICHAEL

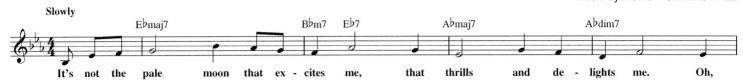

It's not the pale moon that ex - cites me, that thrills and de - lights me. Oh,

no,_____ it's just The Near-ness Of You._____ It is - n't your sweet con - ver -

sa - tion that brings this sen - sa - tion. Oh, no,_____ it's just The Near-ness Of

You._____ When you're in my arms_____ and I feel you so

close to me_____ all my wild - est dreams come

true._____ I need no soft lights to en chant me if

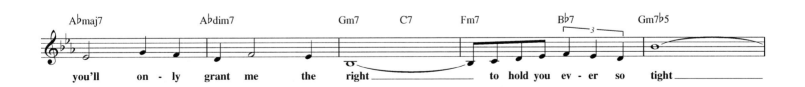

you'll on - ly grant me the right_____ to hold you ev - er so tight_____

_____ and to feel in the night The Near - ness Of You._____

NEVER ON SUNDAY
from Jules Dassin's Motion Picture NEVER ON SUNDAY

Words by BILLY TOWNE
Music by MANOS HADJIDAKIS

NICHOLAS AND ALEXANDRA
Theme from NICHOLAS AND ALEXANDRA

By RICHARD RODNEY BENNETT

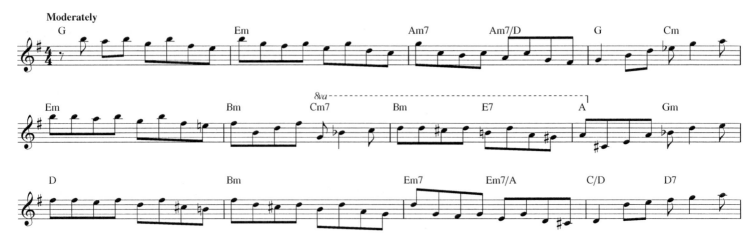

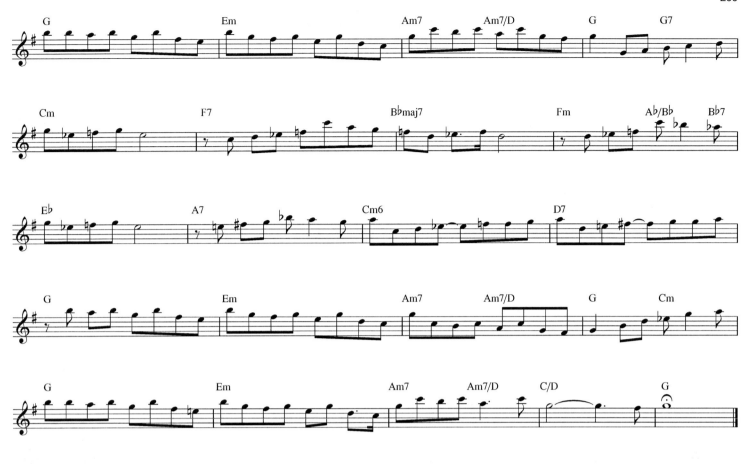

THE NIGHT THEY INVENTED CHAMPAGNE
from GIGI

Words by ALAN JAY LERNER
Music by FREDERICK LOEWE

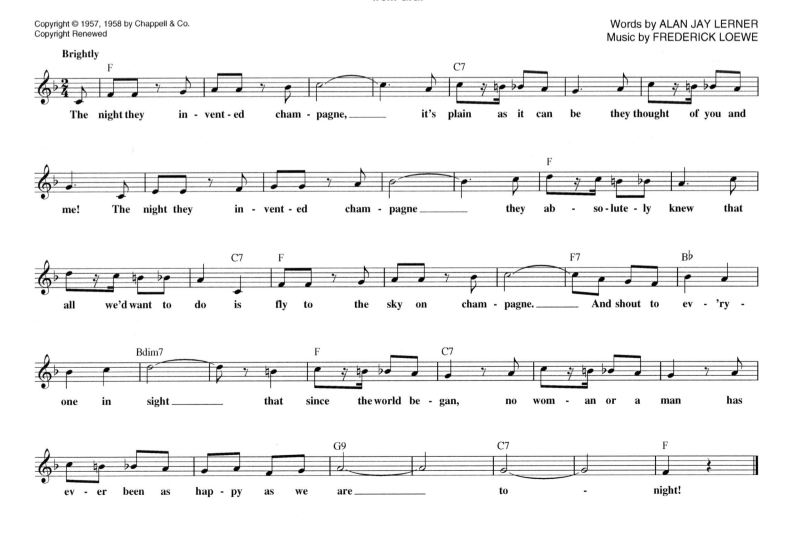

NIGHT FEVER
from SATURDAY NIGHT FEVER

Words and Music by BARRY GIBB,
ROBIN GIBB and MAURICE GIBB

NINE TO FIVE
from NINE TO FIVE

Words and Music by
DOLLY PARTON

Lively

Tum-ble out of bed and stum-ble to the kitch-en; pour my-self a cup___ of am-bi-tion, and
They let you dream just to watch them shat-ter; you're just a step on the boss man's lad-der, but

yawn, and stretch, and try to come___ to life.___ Jump in the show-er, and the
you've got dreams he'll nev-er take___ a-way.___ In the same boat with a

blood starts pump-ing; out on the street, the traf-fic starts jump-ing, with folks___ like me on the
lot of your friends; wait-in' for the day your___ ship-'ll come in, and the tides gon-na turn and

job from nine to five. Work-ing nine to___ five,___ what a
it's all gon-na roll your way. Work-ing nine to___ five,___ for

way to make___ a liv-ing; bare-ly get-ting by,___ it's all tak-ing and___ no
ser-vice and___ de-vo-tion; you would think___ that I___ would de-serve a fair___ pro-

giv-ing. They just use___ your mind,___ and they nev-er give___ you cre-dit; it's e-
mo-tion; want to move___ a-head,___ but the boss won't seem___ to let me. I

1 D7
nough to drive___ you___ cra-zy, if___ you let it.

2 D7
swear some-times,___ that man is out___ to get___ me.

N.C. **D.C. al Coda**

CODA
nine to___ five,___
Nine to___ five,___

___ what a way to make a liv-ing; bare-ly get-ting by,___ it's all
___ they've got you where they want___ you; there's a bet-ter life,___ and you

tak-ing and___ no giv-ing. They just use___ your mind,___ and you nev-er get___ the
dream a-bout___ it don't you? It's a rich___ man's game,___ no mat-ter what___ they

A7 **D7** **Repeat and Fade**
cre-dit; it's e-nough to drive___ you___ cra-zy, if___ you let it.
call it; and you spend your life___ put-ting mon-ey in___ his pock-et.

NO MORE LONELY NIGHTS
from the Motion Picture GIVE MY REGARDS TO BROAD STREET

Words and Music by
PAUL McCARTNEY

(Instrumental)

NO TWO PEOPLE
from the Motion Picture HANS CHRISTIAN ANDERSEN

By FRANK LOESSER

Light n' Lively

Nev-er be-fore and nev-er a-gain could an-y-thing more ro-man-tic and beau-ti-ful be!

No two peo-ple have ev-er been so in love been so in love, been so in love.
No two peo-ple have ev-er mooned such a moon Juned such a June spooned such a spoon.

No two peo-ple have ev-er been so in love as my lov-ey dove and I.
No two peo-ple have ev-er been so in tune as my ma-ca-roon and

I. And when we kiss and when we kiss well, it's his-tor-i-cal, it's hy-ster-i-cal

well, cer-tain-ly dar-ling. No two peo-ple have ev-er been so in love, been so in love,

been so in love. No two peo-ple have ev-er been so in love, as my lov-ey dove and

(This is the cream, the ver-y ex-treme, the sort of a dream you could-n't i-mag-ine at

No two peo-ple have ev-er been so in love as my lov-ey dove and I.
all)

O MIO BABBINO CARO
from A ROOM WITH A VIEW

By GIACOMO PUCCINI

O mio bab-bi-no Ca-ro, mi pia-ce,é bel-lo, bel-lo; vo' an-da-re in Por-ta Ros-sa

a com-pe-rar l'a-nel-lo! Sì, sì, ci voglio an-da-re! E se l'a-mas-si in-dar-no, an-drei sul Pon-te

Vec-chio, ma per but-tar-mi in Ar-no! Mi strug-go e mi tor-men-to! O Di-o, vor-rei mo-

rir! *(Instrumental)* Bab-bo, pie-tà, pie-tà! Bab-bo, pie-tà, pie-tà!

THE ODD COUPLE
Theme from the Paramount Picture THE ODD COUPLE

Words by SAMMY CAHN
Music by NEAL HEFTI

No mat-ter where they go they are known as the cou-ple. They're nev-er seen a-lone

so they're known as the cou-ple. As I've in-di-cat-ed

they are nev-er quite sep-a-rat-ed, they are peas in a pod. Don't you think that it's odd?

Their hab-its, I con-fess, none can guess with the cou-ple. If

one says no it's yes more or less, with the cou-ple. But they're laugh pro-

vok-ing; yet they real-ly don't know they're jok-ing. Don't you find when love is blind it's kind of

odd! No odd! Don't you think it's odd?

Don't you think it's odd? Don't you think it's odd?

OLE BUTTERMILK SKY
from the Motion Picture CANYON PASSAGE

By HOAGY CARMICHAEL
and JACK BROOKS

Moderately

Ole but - ter - milk sky, _____ I'm keep - ing my eye peeled on you. ___ What's the good

word to - night? _____ Are you gon - na be mel - low to - night? _____ Ole but - ter - milk sky, _____

_____ can't you see my lit - tle don - key and me? _____ We're as hap - py as a Christ - mas tree,

head - in' for the one I love. _____ I'm gon - na pop 'er the ques - tion, that

ques - tion, "Do you, dar - lin', do you do." ___ It - 'll be eas - y, so eas - y if

I can on - ly bank on you. ___ Old but - ter - milk sky, _____ I'm tell - ing you why; now you know. ___

Keep it in mind to - night, _____ keep a - brush - ing those clouds _ from sight. _____ Ole but - ter - milk

sky, _____ don't you fail me when I'm need - in' you most. _____ Hang a moon a - bove her hitch - ing post;

Hitch me to the one I love. _____ You can if you try. _____ Don't tell me no

lie. _____ Will you be mel - low and bright to - night, _____ but - ter - milk sky?

OH, PRETTY WOMAN

featured in the Motion Picture PRETTY WOMAN

Words and Music by ROY ORBISON
and BILL DEES

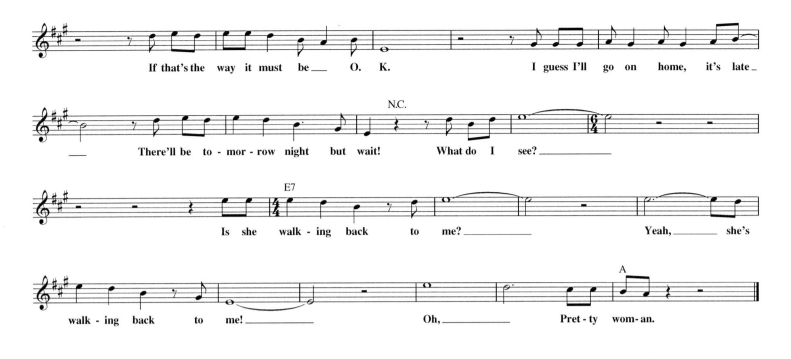

If that's the way it must be ___ O. K. I guess I'll go on home, it's late ___

There'll be to-mor-row night but wait! What do I see? ___

Is she walk-ing back to me? ___ Yeah, ___ she's

walk-ing back to me! ___ Oh, ___ Pret-ty wom-an.

ON BROADWAY
featured in the Motion Picture A CHORUS LINE

© 1962, 1963 (Renewed 1990, 1991) SCREEN GEMS-EMI MUSIC INC.

Words and Music by BARRY MANN,
CYNTHIA WEIL, MIKE STOLLER
and JERRY LEIBER

Moderately

They say the ne-on lights are bright) on Broad-way; ___
They say the wom-en treat you fine ___ }
They say that I won't last too long ___)

They say there's al-ways mag-ic in the air.
But look-in' at them just gives me ___ the blues.
I'll catch a Grey-hound bus for home, ___ they say.

But when you're walk-in' down the street, And you ain't had e-nough to eat, ___
'Cause how ya gon-na make some time, ___ When all you got is one thin dime, ___
But they're dead wrong, I know they are, ___ 'cause I can play this here gui-tar, ___

The glit-ter rubs right off and you're ___ no-where. ___
And one thin dime won't e-ven shine your shoes. ___
And I won't quit till

I'm a star ___ on Broad-way. ___

ON GOLDEN POND
Main Theme from ON GOLDEN POND

Music by DAVE GRUSIN

ONE FOR MY BABY (AND ONE MORE FOR THE ROAD)

from the Motion Picture THE SKY'S THE LIMIT

Lyric by JOHNNY MERCER
Music by HAROLD ARLEN

Lazily

It's quart-er to three,— there's no one in the place ex-cept you and me._____ So,

set 'em up Joe,— I've got a lit-tle sto-ry you ought-a know._____ We're

drink-ing, my friend,— to the end— of a brief ep-i-sode._____ Make it

one for my ba-by and one more for the road. I

got the rou-tine,— so drop an-oth-er nick-el in the ma-chine._____ I'm
that's how it goes— and Joe, I know you're get-ting anx-ious to close._____ So,

feel-in' so bad,— I wish you'd make the mu-sic dream-y and sad._____ Could
thanks for the cheer,— I hope you did-n't mind my bend-ing your ear._____ This

tell you a lot,— but you've got____ to be true to your code._____ Make it
torch that I've found,— must be drowned_ or it might ex-plode._____

one for my ba-by and one more for the road. You'd nev-er know it, but

Bud-dy, I'm a kind of po-et and I've got-ta lot-ta things to say. And

when I'm gloom-y, you sim-ply got-ta lis-ten to me, un-til it's talked a-way. Well,

CODA

road, that long, long road._____

ON THE GOOD SHIP LOLLIPOP
from BRIGHT EYES

Words and Music by SIDNEY CLARE
and RICHARD A. WHITING

ONCE UPON A DREAM
from Walt Disney's SLEEPING BEAUTY

Words and Music by SAMMY FAIN
and JACK LAWRENCE
Adapted from a Theme by TCHAIKOVSKY

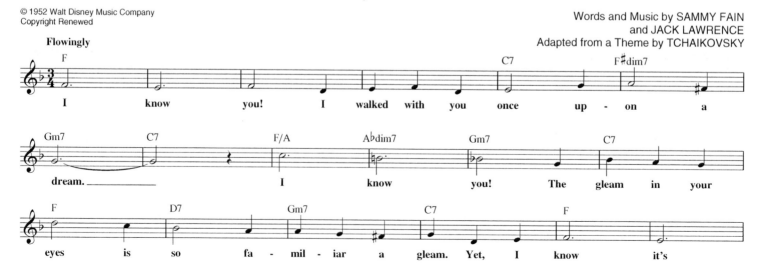

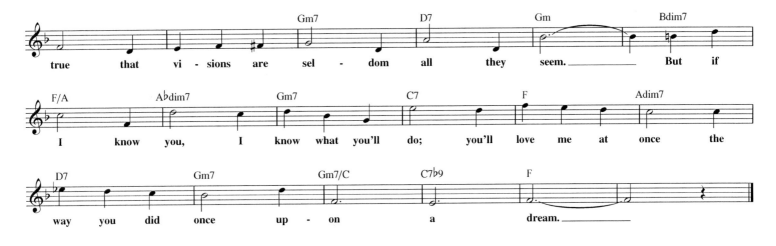

ONE TIN SOLDIER
from BILLY JACK

Words and Music by DENNIS LAMBERT
and BRIAN POTTER

ONLY HOPE

from the Warner Bros. Motion Picture A WALK TO REMEMBER

Words and Music by
JONATHAN FOREMAN

THEME FROM "ORDINARY PEOPLE"

Arranged by
MARVIN HAMLISCH

Or - di - nar - y   peo - ple ___

Or - di - nar - y   peo - ple ___

PARIS IS A LONELY TOWN
from the Motion Picture GAY PURR-EE

Lyric by E.Y. HARBURG
Music by HAROLD ARLEN

The glam-our's gone, the shades are down and Par-is is on-ly a lone-ly town, lone-ly! _____ When

love's a laugh and you're the clown, then Par-is is on-ly a drear-y town, drear-y! _____

For the love-less clown this town's a wea-ry mer-ry-go-round and round and round. The

chest-nut, the wil-low, the col-ors of U-tril-lo turn to grey, grey hues, The band play-ing Bi-zet, a-

long the Champs El-y-see, sounds like way down blues. Par-is is a drear-y,

lone-ly, oh! so lone-ly town. _____ Where's that shin-ing flow-er 'neath the Eif-fel Tow-er?

Where's that fair-y land of gold? _ Is-n't it a pit-y that this mag-ic cit-y

turned sud-den-ly cold! The chim-neys moan, the riv-er cries, each glam-or-ous bridge is a bridge of sighs;

Riv-er, riv-er, won't you be my lov-er? Don't _____ turn me down for

Par-is is such a lone-ly, lone-ly town. _____

PART OF YOUR WORLD
from Walt Disney's THE LITTLE MERMAID

Lyrics by HOWARD ASHMAN
Music by ALAN MENKEN

PASS ME BY
from the Motion Picture FATHER GOOSE

Lyric by CAROLYN LEIGH
Music by CY COLEMAN

PENNIES FROM HEAVEN
from PENNIES FROM HEAVEN

Words by JOHN BURKE
Music by ARTHUR JOHNSTON

PERSONALITY
from THE ROAD TO UTOPIA

Words by JOHNNY BURKE
Music by JIMMY VAN HEUSEN

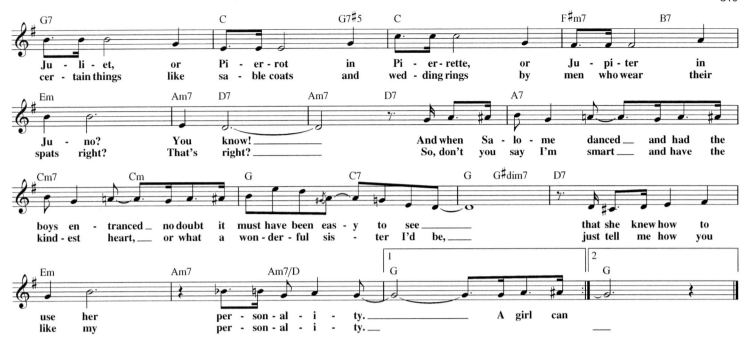

PICK YOURSELF UP
from SWING TIME

Words by DOROTHY FIELDS
Music by JEROME KERN

PICNIC
from the Columbia Technicolor Picture PICNIC

Words by STEVE ALLEN
Music by GEORGE W. DUNING

PILLOW TALK
from PILLOW TALK

Words and Music by INEZ JAMES
and BUDDY PEPPER

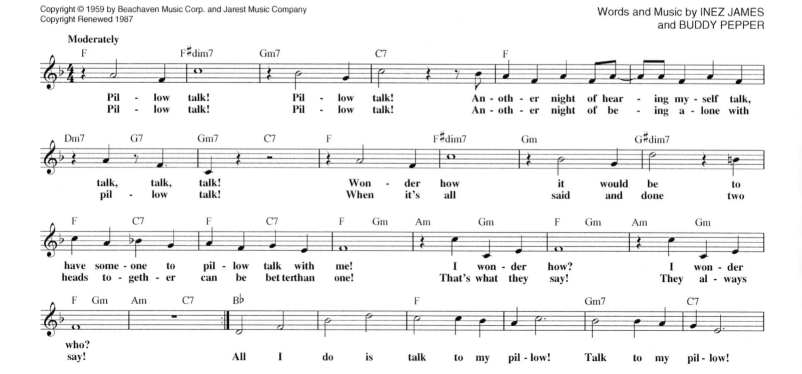

A PLACE IN THE SUN
(Tonight My Love)
from the Paramount Motion Picture A PLACE IN THE SUN

Words by JAY LIVINGSTON and RAY EVANS
Music by FRANZ WAXMAN

A PRAYER FOR PEACE
from MUNICH

Music by JOHN WILLIAMS

QUANDO MEN VO
(Musetta's Waltz)
featured in the Motion Picture MOONSTRUCK

By GIACOMO PUCCINI

THE PROMISE
(I'll Never Say Goodbye)
Theme from the Universal Motion Picture THE PROMISE

Words by ALAN and MARILYN BERGMAN
Music by DAVID SHIRE

PSYCHO
(Prelude)
Theme from the Paramount Picture PSYCHO

Music by BERNARD HERRMANN

PUTTIN' ON THE RITZ

from the Motion Picture PUTTIN' ON THE RITZ
featured in YOUNG FRANKENSTEIN

Words and Music by
IRVING BERLIN

QUE SERA, SERA
(Whatever Will Be, Will Be)
from THE MAN WHO KNEW TOO MUCH

Words and Music by JAY LIVINGSTON
and RAY EVANS

RAINDROPS KEEP FALLIN' ON MY HEAD
from BUTCH CASSIDY AND THE SUNDANCE KID

Lyric by HAL DAVID
Music by BURT BACHARACH

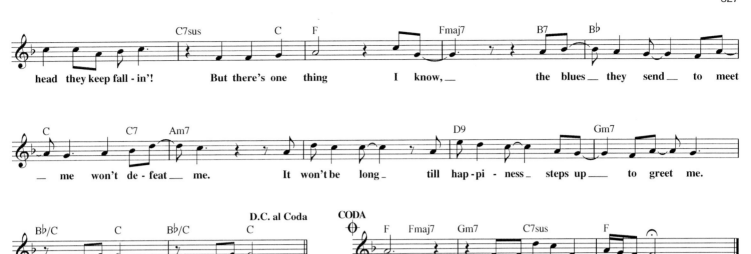

READY TO TAKE A CHANCE AGAIN

(Love Theme)
from the Paramount Picture FOUL PLAY

Words by NORMAN GIMBEL
Music by CHARLES FOX

THE RAINBOW CONNECTION
from THE MUPPET MOVIE

Words and Music by PAUL WILLIAMS
and KENNETH L. ASCHER

Additional Lyrics

3. Have you been half asleep and have you heard voices?
I've heard them calling my name.
Is this the sweet sound that calls the young sailors?
The voice might be one and the same.
I've heard it too many times to ignore it.
It's something that I'm s'posed to be.
Someday we'll find it,
The rainbow connection,
The lovers, the dreamers and me.

REFLECTION
from Walt Disney Pictures' MULAN

Music by MATTHEW WILDER
Lyrics by DAVID ZIPPEL

REMEMBER ME THIS WAY
from the Universal Motion Picture CASPER

Music by DAVID FOSTER
Lyrics by LINDA THOMPSON

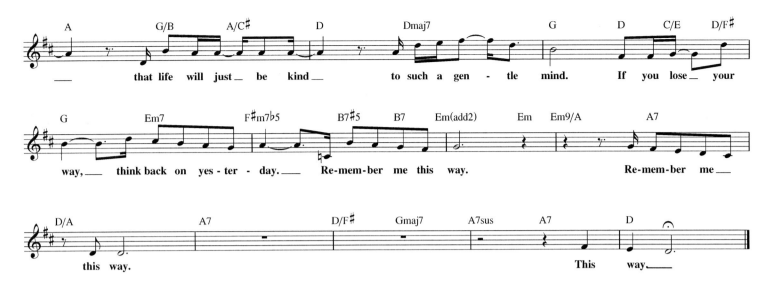

RIDE OF THE VALKYRIES

featured in the Motion Picture APOCALYPSE NOW

By RICHARD WAGNER

(GHOST) RIDERS IN THE SKY

(A Cowboy Legend)

from RIDERS IN THE SKY

By STAN JONES

THE RIVER KWAI MARCH
from THE BRIDGE ON THE RIVER KWAI

By MALCOLM ARNOLD

RIVER
from the Motion Picture THE MISSION

Music by ENNIO MORRICONE

ROCK AROUND THE CLOCK
featured in the Motion Picture AMERICAN GRAFFITI
featured in the Motion Picture BLACKBOARD JUNGLE

Words and Music by MAX C. FREEDMAN
and JIMMY DeKNIGHT

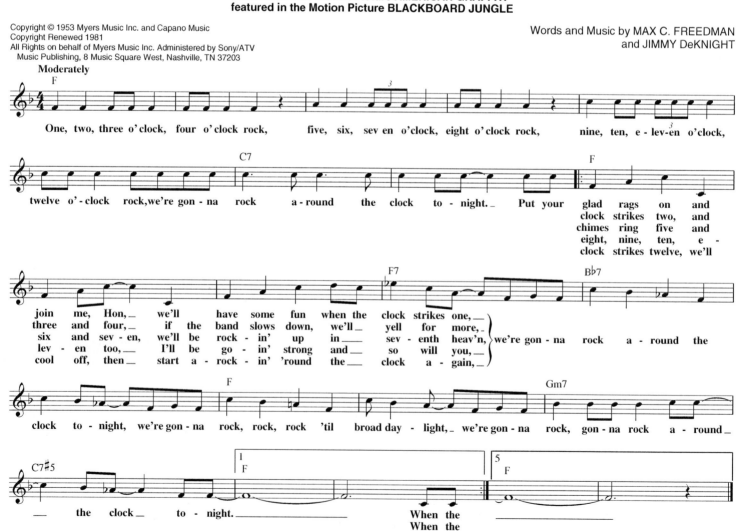

ROSALIE
from ROSALIE

Words and Music by
COLE PORTER

MAIN TITLE
Theme from RUDY

Composed by JERRY GOLDSMITH

SAN ANTONIO ROSE
from SAN ANTONIO ROSE

By BOB WILLS

SAYURI'S THEME
from MEMOIRS OF A GEISHA

By JOHN WILLIAMS

SAY YOU, SAY ME
from the Motion Picture WHITE NIGHTS

Words and Music by
LIONEL RICHIE

THEME FROM "SCHINDLER'S LIST"
(Reprise)
from the Universal Motion Picture SCHINDLER'S LIST

Composed by JOHN WILLIAMS

SEA OF LOVE

Words and Music by GEORGE KHOURY
and PHILIP BAPTISTE

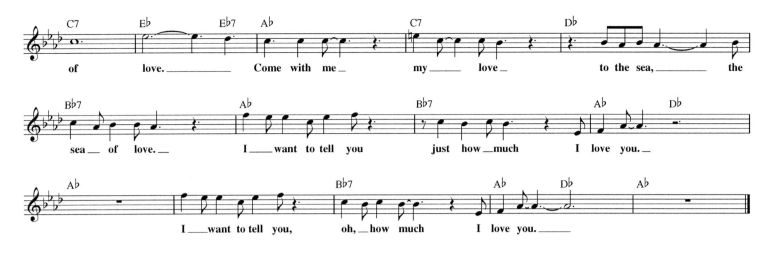

of love. Come with me my love to the sea, the sea of love. I want to tell you just how much I love you. I want to tell you, oh, how much I love you.

THE SEDUCTION
(Love Theme)
from the Paramount Motion Picture AMERICAN GIGOLO

Music by GIORGIO MORODER

SEASONS OF LOVE
from RENT

Words and Music by
JONATHAN LARSON

way that she died. _____ It's time now to sing out, though the sto-ry nev-er ends. _____ Let's

cel-e-brate, re-mem-ber a year in the life of ___ friends. _ Re-mem-ber the love,

_____ re-mem-ber the love, re-mem-ber the

love, _____ meas-ure in love. _____ Sea-sons of

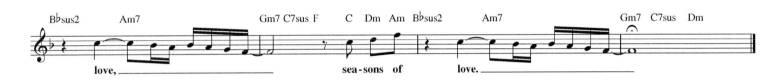

love, _____ sea-sons of love. _____

SEEMS LIKE OLD TIMES
from ARTHUR GODFREY AND HIS FRIENDS

Lyric and Music by JOHN JACOB LOEB
and CARMEN LOMBARDO

Moderately

Seems like old times, hav-ing you to walk with, seems like old times,
old times, din-ner dates and flow-ers, just like old times,

hav-ing you to talk with. And it's still a thrill just to have my arms a-
stay-ing up for hours. Mak-ing dreams come true, do-ing things we used to

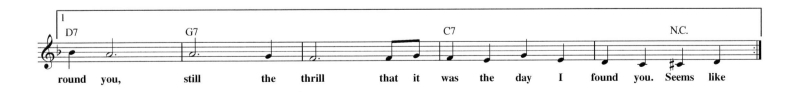

round you, still the thrill that it was the day I found you. Seems like

do, seems like old times, _____ be-ing here with you. _____

SEIZE THE DAY
from Walt Disney's NEWSIES

Lyrics by JACK FLEDMAN
Music by ALAN MENKEN

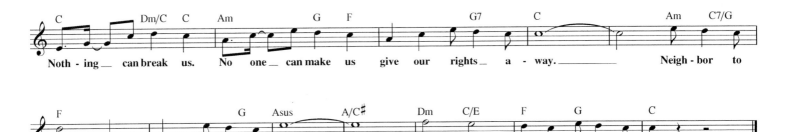

SHE
from NOTTING HILL

Lyric by HERBERT KRETZMER
Music by CHARLES AZNAVOUR

THEME FROM SHAFT
from SHAFT

Words and Music by
ISAAC HAYES

Moderate Funk Rock

(Spoken:) Who's the black private dick

SEPARATE LIVES
Love Theme from WHITE NIGHTS

Words and Music by
STEPHEN BISHOP

SISTERS
from the Motion Picture Irving Berlin's WHITE CHRISTMAS

Words and Music by
IRVING BERLIN

SING, YOU SINNERS

from the Paramount Picture HONEY
Theme from the Paramount Picture SING, YOU SINNERS

Words and Music by SAM COSLOW
and W. FRANKE HARLING

SOME DAY MY PRINCE WILL COME

from Walt Disney's SNOW WHITE AND THE SEVEN DWARFS

Words by LARRY MOREY
Music by FRANK CHURCHILL

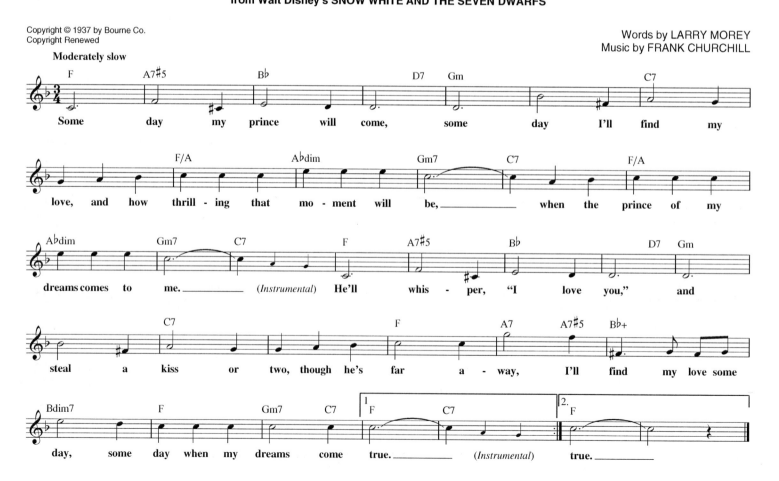

SOMEDAY
from Walt Disney's THE HUNCHBACK OF NOTRE DAME

Music by ALAN MENKEN
Lyrics by STEPHEN SCHWARTZ

SOMEONE'S WAITING FOR YOU
from Walt Disney's THE RESCUERS

Words by CAROL CONNORS and AYN ROBBINS
Music by SAMMY FAIN

Be brave lit-tle one. Make a wish for each sad lit-tle tear. Hold your head up though

no one is near. Some-one's wait-ing for you. ____ Don't

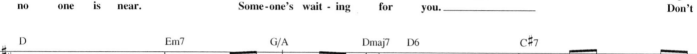

cry lit-tle one. There'll be a smile where a frown used to be. You'll be part of the

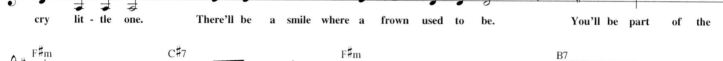

love that you see. Some-one's wait-ing for you. ____ Al - ways keep a lit-tle prayer in your

pock - et and you're sure to see the light. Soon there'll be joy and hap-pi - ness and

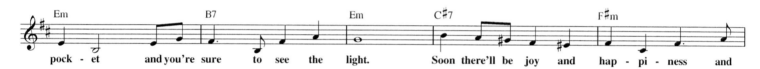

your lit - tle world will be bright. Have faith lit - tle one ____ 'til your hopes and your

wish - es come true. You must try to be brave lit - tle one. ____ Some - one's

wait - ing to love you. ____ Be you. ____

SOMETHING GOOD
from THE SOUND OF MUSIC

Lyrics and Music by
RICHARD RODGERS

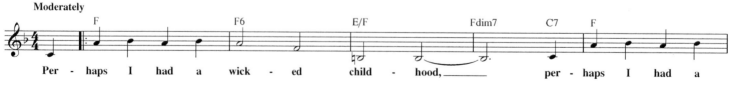

Per - haps I had a wick - ed child - hood, ____ per - haps I had a

mis - 'ra - ble youth. ____ But some-where in my wick - ed mis - 'ra - ble past ____ there

must have been a mo-ment of truth._____ For here you are, stand-ing there,

lov-ing me,_____ wheth-er or not you should._____ So, some-where in my

youth or child-hood_____ I must have done some-thing good._____ Per-

good._____ Noth-ing comes from noth-ing, noth-ing ev-er could. So, some-where in my

youth or child-hood_____ I must have done some-thing good._____

SOMEWHERE IN MY MEMORY
from the Twentieth Century Fox Motion Picture HOME ALONE

Words by LESLIE BRICUSSE
Music by JOHN WILLIAMS

Gently and with simplicity

Can-dles in the win-dow, shad-ows paint-ing the ceil-ing, gaz-ing at the

fire glow, feel-ing that "gin-ger-bread" feel-ing. Pre-cious mo-ments,

spe-cial peo-ple, hap-py fac-es I can see. Some-where in my mem-'ry,

Christ-mas joys all a-round me, liv-ing in my mem-'ry, all of the mu-sic,

all of the mag-ic, all of the fam-'ly home here with me._____

SOMETHING TO TALK ABOUT
(Let's Give Them Something to Talk About)
from SOMETHING TO TALK ABOUT

Words and Music by
SHIRLEY EIKHARD

you just fig-ure out. _____ Give them some-thing to talk a-bout. How a-bout

love? _____ wooh, ___ lis-ten up, ba-by. A lit-tle mys t'ry won't hurt. _

Give them some-thing to talk a-bout. How a-bout_ love?___

(Instrumental)

SOMEWHERE IN TIME
from SOMEWHERE IN TIME

By JOHN BARRY

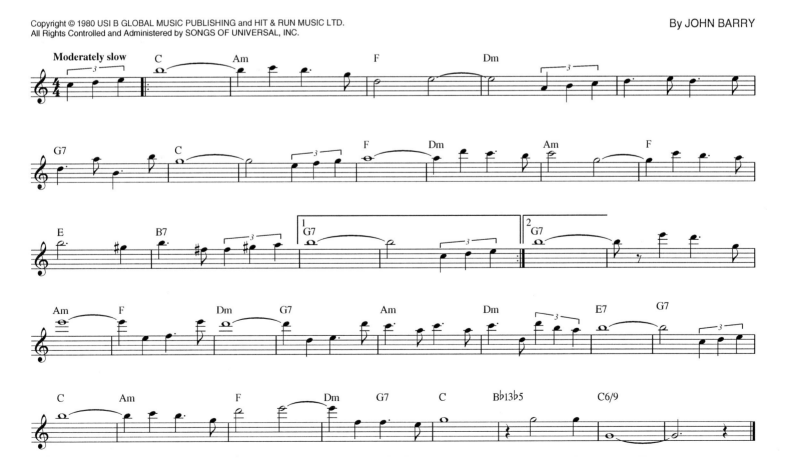

SOMEWHERE, MY LOVE
Lara's Theme from DOCTOR ZHIVAGO

Lyric by PAUL FRANCIS WEBSTER
Music by MAURICE JARRE

Moderately, with expression

Some - where, my love, there will be songs to sing, al - though the snow
cov - ers the hope of spring. Some - where a hill blos - soms in green and gold,
and there are dreams all that your heart can hold. Some - day ____ we'll meet a -
gain, my love. Some - day ____ when - ev - er the spring breaks through.
You'll come to me out of the long a - go, warm as the wind soft as the kiss of
snow. { Till then, my sweet, } think of me now and then. God - speed, my love,
{ (Lar - a, my own) }
'til you are mine a - gain. 'til you are mine ____ a - gain. ____

SONNY BOY
from THE SINGING FOOL

Words and Music by AL JOLSON, B.G. DeSYLVA,
LEW BROWN and RAY HENDERSON

Moderately

When there are gray skies, I don't mind the gray skies, you make them blue, Son - ny Boy. ____
Friends may for - sake me, let them all for - sake me, you'll pull me through, Son - ny
Boy. You're sent from heav - en, and I know your worth. You've made a
heav - en for me right here on earth. { When I'm old and gray, dear, prom - ise you won't
And then the an - gels grew lone - ly, took you 'cause they're
stray, dear, I love you so, Son - ny Boy. ____
lone - ly, now I'm lone - ly too, Son - ny Boy. ____

Somewhere Out There

from AN AMERICAN TAIL

Music by BARRY MANN and JAMES HORNER
Lyric by CYNTHIA WEIL

Moderately, with expression

Some-where out there be-neath the pale moon-light some-one's think-in' of me and

lov-ing me to-night. Some-where out there some-one's say-ing a prayer that

we'll find one an-oth-er in that big some-where out there. And e-ven though I know how ver-y

far a-part we are it helps to think we might be wish-in' on the same bright star. And

when the night wind starts to sing that lone-some lull-a-by it helps to think we're sleep-ing un-der-neath the same big

sky. Some-where out there if love can see us through, then we'll be to-geth-er some-where

out there, out where dreams come true. (Instrumenal)

D.S. al Coda

And love can see us through, then we'll be to-
(love can see us through)

geth-er some-where out there, out where dreams come true.

SONG OF THE SOUTH
from Walt Disney's SONG OF THE SOUTH

Words by SAM COSLOW
Music by ARTHUR JOHNSTON

Slowly

I hear the mur-mur of the south-wind and feel a half-re-mem-bered thrill, Plain-tive ech-oes faint-ly cling-ing, an old plan-ta-tion air is still ring-ing.

Slowly, with nostalgia

Song Of The South, your mu-sic weaves a mag-ic spell, Song Of The South, I see the scenes I know so well, Cot-ton-woods in blos-som o-ver my cab-in door, Pale moon-light on a field of white, You bring them back once more. I seem to hear those gen-tle voic-es call-ing low, Out of the long long a-go. This heart of mine is in the heart of Dix-ie, that's where I be-long, Sing-ing a song, a Song Of The South.

SOON
from the Paramount Picture MISSISSIPPI

Words by LORENZ HART
Music by RICHARD RODGERS

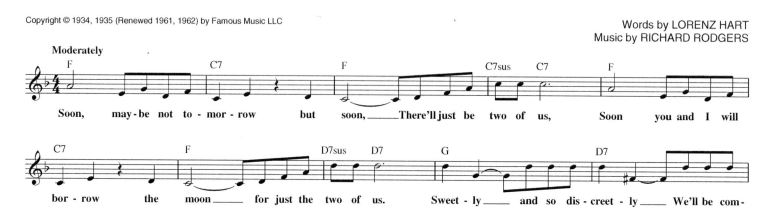

Moderately

Soon, may-be not to-mor-row but soon, There'll just be two of us, Soon you and I will bor-row the moon for just the two of us. Sweet-ly and so dis-creet-ly We'll be com-

plete - ly a - lone; No oth - er world, On - ly our own. Now we must be con - tent - ed with schemes __ a - bout the two of us. Yet we can have our sweet scent - ed dreams, __ That will come true of us, for pres - ent - ly and pleas ant - ly our hearts will be in tune. So, soon, may be not to - mor - row, but soon. __ soon. __

THEME FROM "SOPHIE'S CHOICE"
from SOPHIE'S CHOICE

By MARVIN HAMLISCH

Slowly, in a flowing 3 (♩. = 1 beat)

SOONER OR LATER (I ALWAYS GET MY MAN)

from the Film DICK TRACY

Words and Music by
STEPHEN SONDHEIM

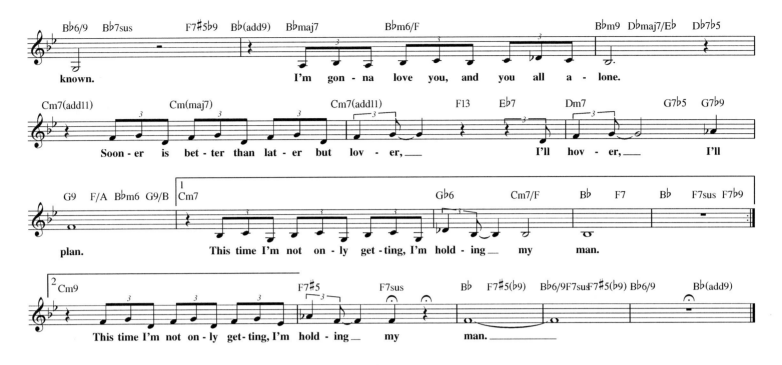

SPARTACUS - LOVE THEME
from the Universal-International Picture Release SPARTACUS

By ALEX NORTH

SPEAK SOFTLY, LOVE
(Love Theme)
from the Paramount Picture THE GODFATHER

Words by LARRY KUSIK
Music by NINO ROTA

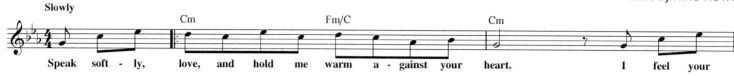

Speak soft-ly, love, and hold me warm a-gainst your heart. I feel your

words, the ten-der, trem-bling mo-ments start. We're in a world our ver-y own, shar-ing a

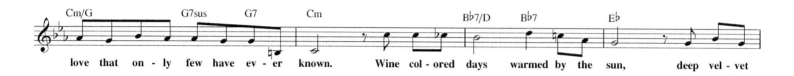

love that on-ly few have ev-er known. Wine col-ored days warmed by the sun, deep vel-vet

nights when we are one. Speak soft-ly, love, so no one hears us but the

sky. The vows of love we make will live un-til we die. My life is yours and all be-

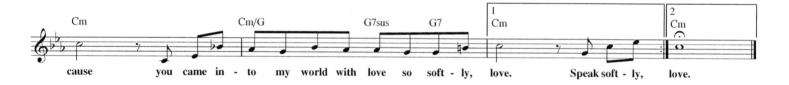

cause you came in-to my world with love so soft-ly, love. Speak soft-ly, love.

A SPOONFUL OF SUGAR
from Walt Disney's MARY POPPINS

Words and Music by RICHARD M. SHERMAN
and ROBERT B. SHERMAN

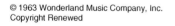

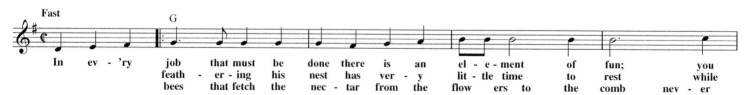

In ev-'ry job that must be done there is an el-e-ment of fun; you
feath-er-ing his nest has ver-y lit-tle time to rest while
bees that fetch the nec-tar from the flow-ers to the comb nev-er

find the fun and snap! the job's a game; And ev-'ry task you un-der-take be-
gath-er-ing his bits of twine and twig. Though quite in-tent in his pur-suit he has a
tire of ev-er buzz-ing to and fro. Be-cause they take a lit-tle nip from ev-'ry

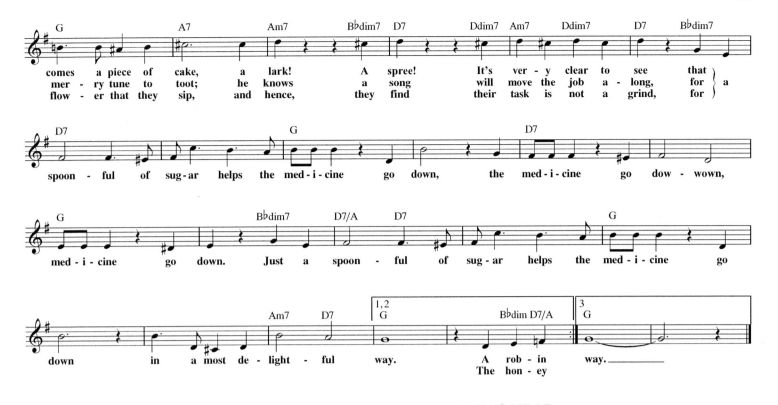

comes a piece of cake, a lark! A spree! It's ver-y clear to see that
mer-ry tune to toot; he knows a song will move the job a-long, for a
flow-er that they sip, and hence, they find their task is not a grind, for

spoon-ful of sug-ar helps the med-i-cine go down, the med-i-cine go dow-wown,

med-i-cine go down. Just a spoon-ful of sug-ar helps the med-i-cine go

down in a most de-light-ful way. A rob-in way.
The hon-ey

SPRING WILL BE A LITTLE LATE THIS YEAR
from the Motion Picture CHRISTMAS HOLIDAY

By FRANK LOESSER

Spring will be a lit-tle late this year, a lit-tle late ar-

riv-ing in my lone-ly world o-ver here. For you have left me, and

where is our A-pril of old? You have left me, and win-ter con-tin-ues

cold, as if to say Spring will be a lit-tle slow to start, a lit-tle

slow re-viv-ing that mu-sic it made in my heart. Yes, time heals

all things, so I need-n't cling to this fear, it's mere-ly that Spring will

be a lit-tle late this year. year.

SPRINGTIME FOR HITLER

Music and Lyrics by
MEL BROOKS

LOVE THEME FROM ST. ELMO'S FIRE
from the Motion Picture ST. ELMO'S FIRE

Words and Music by
DAVID FOSTER

Moderately slow

STAND BY ME
featured in the Motion Picture STAND BY ME

Words and Music by JERRY LEIBER,
MIKE STOLLER and BEN E. KING

Slowly

When the night ___ has come and the land is dark and the moon ___ is the on-ly ___ light we'll

see. No, I won't be a-fraid, no I ___ won't be a-fraid just as

long ___ as you stand, ___ stand by me. So, dar-ling, dar-ling, stand ___ by me, oh, ___

stand ___ by me. Oh, stand, ___ stand by me, stand by me. ___ If the

sea ___ that we look up - on should tum - ble and fall or the moun - tain ___ should

crum - ble ___ in the sea, I won't cry, I won't cry, no ___ I ___

won't shed a tear just as long ___ as you stand, ___ stand by me. So, dar - ling, dar - ling,

STAR TREK® GENERATIONS
Theme from the Paramount Motion Picture STAR TREK: GENERATIONS

Music by DENNIS McCARTHY

STAR TREK® – THE MOTION PICTURE
Theme from the Paramount Picture STAR TREK: THE MOTION PICTURE

Music by JERRY GOLDSMITH

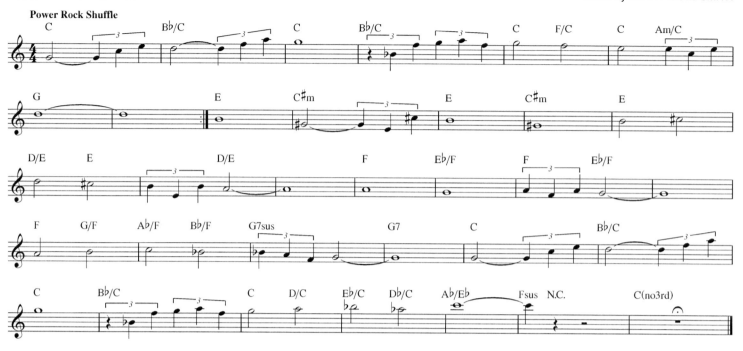

STAR TREK® III - THE SEARCH FOR SPOCK
Theme from the Paramount Motion Picture STAR TREK III: THE SEARCH FOR SPOCK

Music by JAMES HORNER

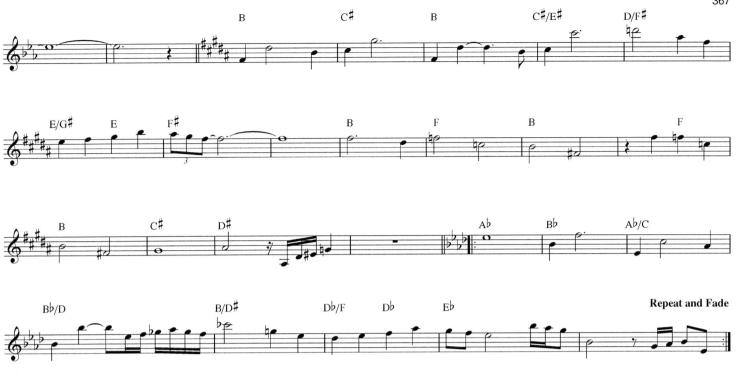

STAR TREK® VI - THE UNDISCOVERED COUNTRY
Suite from the Paramount Motion Picture STAR TREK VI: THE UNDISCOVERED COUNTRY

Music by CLIFF EIDELMAN

STAR TREK® IV: THE VOYAGE HOME
Theme from the Paramount Motion Picture STAR TREK IV: THE VOYAGE HOME

Music by ALEXANDER COURAGE
and LEONARD ROSENMAN

STAR TREK® II: THE WRATH OF KHAN
Theme from the Paramount Motion Picture STAR TREK II: THE WRATH OF KHAN

Music by ALEXANDER COURAGE
and JAMES HORNER

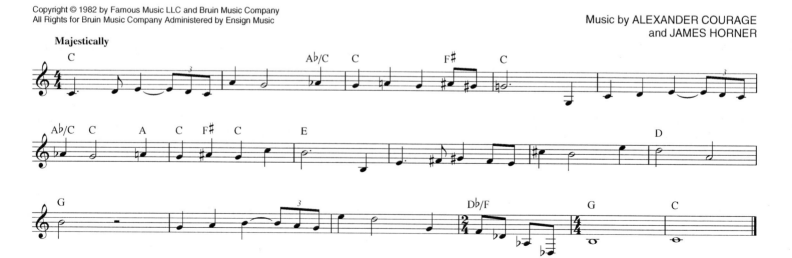

STAYIN' ALIVE

from the Motion Picture SATURDAY NIGHT FEVER

Words and Music by BARRY GIBB,
ROBIN GIBB and MAURICE GIBB

Medium Rock beat

Well, you can tell ____ by the way I use ____ my walk, I'm a wom - an's man: no time to talk. ____
____ get ____ low and I ____ get high and if I ____ can't get ei - ther, I real - ly try. Got the

Mu - sic loud ____ and wom - en warm ____ I've been kicked a - round ____ since I ____ was born. And now it's
wings of heav - en on ____ my shoes, I'm a danc - in' man ____ and I just can't lose. You know it's

all right. ____ It's O. K. ____ And you may look ____ the oth - er way. ____
all right. ____ It's O. K. ____ I'll live to see ____ an - oth - er day. ____

We can try ____ to un - der - stand ____ the New York Times' ef - fect ____ on man. ____

Wheth - er you're a broth - er or wheth - er you're a moth - er, you're stay - in' a - live, ____ stay - in' a - live. ____

Feel the cit - y break - in' and ev - 'ry - bod - y shak - in' and we're stay - in' a - live, ____ stay - in' a - live. ____

Ah, ha, ha, ha, stay - in' a - live, ____ stay - in' a - live. ____ Ah, ha, ha, ha,

stay - in' a - live. ____

1.
Well now, I ____

2.
Life go - in' no - where. ____ Some - bod - y help me. ____

Some - bod - y help ____ me, yeah. ____

Life go - in' no - where. ____

D.S. and Fade

Some - bod - y help ____ me, yeah. ____ Stay - in' a - live. ____ Well, you can tell ____

STARTING OVER
(Love Theme)
from the Paramount Motion Picture STARTING OVER

Words by CAROLE BAYER SAGER
Music by MARVIN HAMLISCH

STELLA BY STARLIGHT
from the Paramount Picture THE UNINVITED

Words by NED WASHINGTON
Music by VICTOR YOUNG

STEPPIN' OUT WITH MY BABY
from the Motion Picture Irving Berlin's EASTER PARADE

Words and Music by
IRVING BERLIN

Medium Jump tempo

If I seem to scin-til-late __ it's be-cause I've got a date, __ a date with a pack-age of __ the good things that come with love. __ You don't have to ask me, __ I won't waste your time. But if you should ask me __ why I feel sub-lime, I'm __ step-pin' out __ / Step-pin' out __ with my ba - by. Can't go wrong __ 'cause I'm in right. It's for sure, __ not for may - be, that I'm all dressed up to-night. __ Step-pin' out __ with my hon-ey, can't be bad __ to feel so good. __ Nev-er felt __ quite so sun-ny, and I keep on knock-in' wood. __ There'll be smooth sail-in' 'cause I'm trim-min' my sails, __ { Male: in my top hat __ and my white tie __ and my / Female: with a bright shine __ on my shoes and __ on my tails. __ / nails. __ } Step-pin' out __ with my ba-by. Can't go wrong __ 'cause I'm in right. Ask me when __ will the day __ be, the big day may be to-night. __ be to-night. __

STORMY WEATHER
(Keeps Rainin' All the Time)
from COTTON CLUB PARADE OF 1933

Lyric by TED KOEHLER
Music by HAROLD ARLEN

STRANGERS IN THE NIGHT
adapted from A MAN COULD GET KILLED

Words by CHARLES SINGLETON and EDDIE SNYDER
Music by BERT KAEMPFERT

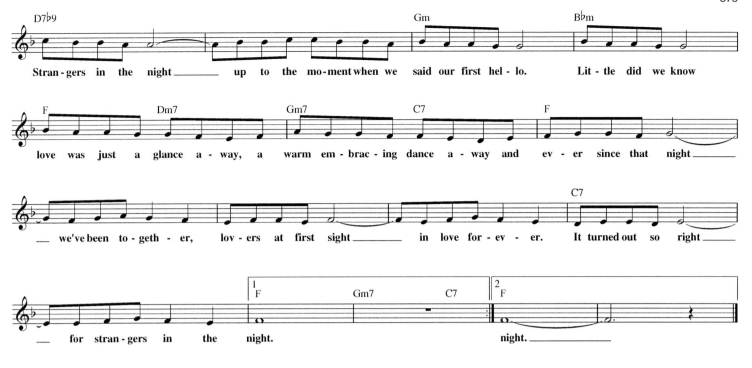

Strangers in the night ____ up to the mo-ment when we said our first hel - lo. Lit - tle did we know love was just a glance a - way, a warm em - brac - ing dance a - way and ev - er since that night ____ __ we've been to - geth - er, lov - ers at first sight ____ in love for - ev - er. It turned out so right ____ __ for stran - gers in the night. night. ____

THE STRIPPER
from THE STRIPPER

Music by DAVID ROSE

STUCK IN THE MIDDLE WITH YOU

Words and Music by GERRY RAFFERTY
and JOE EGAN

Moderately

Well, I don't know why I came here to-night. I got the
Stuck in the mid-dle with you and I'm won-
Tryin' to make some sense of it all
Instrumental

feel-in' that some-thing ain't right. I'm so scared in case I fall off my chair
-d'ring what it is I should do. It's so hard to keep this smile from my face.
see it makes no sense at all. Is it cool to go to sleep on the floor?

and I'm won-d'ring how I'll get down the stairs.
Los-ing con-trol I'm all o-ver the place. (1.-3.) Clowns
You don't think that I can take an-y-more. *Instrumental*

to the left of me, jok-ers to the right. Here I am, stuck in the mid-dle with you.

1,3
(Yes, I'm *Instrumental* *Instrumental ends*) Well, you start-ed out with lov-in' and you found that you're a self-made man.
2,4

And you fan-cy I'll come crawl-in' slap you on the back and say

Am/D
please, please. To Coda

D.S. al Coda
(with repeat)

CODA
D
(Instrumental)

And I don't

know why I came here to-night. I got the feel-in' that some-thing ain't right. I'm so scared

G7
in case I fall off my chair and I'm won-d'ring how I'll get down the stairs. Clowns
D

SUMMERTIME IN VENICE
from the Motion Picture SUMMERTIME

English Words by CARL SIGMAN
Music by ALESSANDRO CICOGNINI

SUMMER NIGHTS
from GREASE

Lyric and Music by WARREN CASEY
and JIM JACOBS

Moderately

Boy: "Sum-mer lov-in,' had me a blast." ___ Girl: "Sum-mer lov-in' hap-pened so fast." ___
"She swam by me; she got a cramp." _ "He ran by me; got my suit damp." ___
"Took her bowl-ing in the ar-cade." ___ "We went stroll-ing; drank lem-on-ade." ___

Boy: "Met a girl, cra-zy for me." _____ Girl: "Met a boy, cute as can be." ___
"Saved her life; she near-ly drowned." _ "He showed off, splash-ing a-round." _
"We made out un-der the dock." ___ "We stayed out till ten o'-clock." _

Sum-mer days drift-ing a-way ___ to, ___ uh, oh, those sum-mer nights. _ Well-a, well-a, well-a
Sum-mer sun, some-thing's be-gun. ___ But, _ uh, oh, those sum-mer nights. _ Well-a, well-a, well-a
Sum-mer fling don't mean a thing. But,

uh. Tell me more. Tell me more. Did you get ver-y far? ___ Tell me more. Tell me more. Like, does he have a car? ___
uh. Tell me more. Tell me more. Was it love at first sight? _ Tell me more. Tell me more. Did she put up a fight? ___

___ uh, oh, those sum-mer nights. ___ Tell me more, tell me

more. But you don't got to brag. ___ Tell me more, tell me more. 'Cause he sounds like a drag. ___

Shu-da bop bop. Shu-da bop bop. Shu-da bop bop. Shu-da bop bop. Girl: "He got friend-ly,

hold-ing my hand." ___ Boy: "She got friend-ly, down in the sand." _____ Girl: "He was sweet;

just turned eight-een." _ Boy: "She was good. You know what I mean." _ Sum-mer heat;

boy and girl meet. But, _ uh, oh those sum-mer nights. _ Tell me more. Tell me

more. How much dough did he spend? _ Tell me more. Tell me more. Could she get me a friend?

SWINGING ON A STAR
from GOING MY WAY

Words by JOHNNY BURKE
Music by JIMMY VAN HEUSEN

SUPERCALIFRAGILISTICEXPIALIDOCIOUS
from Walt Disney's MARY POPPINS

Words and Music by RICHARD M. SHERMAN
and ROBERT B. SHERMAN

Brightly

Su-per-cal-i-frag-il-is-tic-ex-pi-al-i-do-cious! E - ven though the

sound of it is some-thing quite a-tro-cious, if you say it loud e-nough, you'll al-ways sound pre-

co-cious. Su-per-cal-i-frag-il-is-tic-ex-pi-al-i-do-cious! Um did-dle did-dle did-dle,

um did-dle ay! Um did-dle did-dle did-dle, um did-dle ay!

Be-cause I was a-fraid to speak when
He trav-eled all a-round the world and
So when the cat has got your tongue, there's

I was just a lad, me fa-ther gave me nose a tweak and told me I was
ev-'ry-where he went he'd use his word and all would say, "There goes a clev-er
no need for dis-may. Just sum-mon up this word and then you've got a lot to

bad. But then one day I learned a word that saved me ach-in' nose, the
gent!" When dukes and ma-'a-ra-jas pass the time of day with me, I
say. But bet-ter use it care-ful-ly or it can change your life. One

big-gest word you ev-er 'eard and this is 'ow it goes: Oh!
say me spe-cial word and then they ask me out to tea. Oh!
night I said it to me girl and now me girl's me wife. She's

(1.,2.) Su-per-cal-i-
(3.) Su-per-cal-i-

frag-il-is-tic-ex-pi-al-i-do-cious! E-ven though the sound of it is
frag-il-is-tic-ex-pi-al-i-do-cious! Su-per-cal-i-frag-il-is-tic-

some-thing quite a-tro-cious, if you say it loud e-nough, you'll al-ways sound pre-
ex-pi-al-i-do-cious! Su-per-cal-i-frag-il-is-tic-ex-pi-al-i-

1, 2 | **3**

co-cious. Su-per-cal-i-frag-il-is-tic-ex-pi-al-i-do-cious!
do-cious! Su-per-cal-i-frag-il-is-tic-ex-pi-al-i- do-cious!

TAKE MY BREATH AWAY
(Love Theme)
from the Paramount Picture TOP GUN

Words and Music by GIORGIO MORODER
and TOM WHITLOCK

Additional Lyrics

2. **Watching, I keep waiting, still anticipating love,**
   Never hesitating to become the fated ones.
   Turning and returning to some secret place to hide;
   Watching in slow motion as you turn to me and say,
   "Take my breath away."
   Bridge

3. **Watching every motion in this foolish lover's game;**
   Haunted by the notion somewhere there's a love in flames.
   Turning and returning to some secret place inside;
   Watching in slow motion as you turn my way and say,
   "Take my breath away."
   Bridge

SWEET SUE–JUST YOU
from RHYTHM PARADE

Words by WILL J. HARRIS
Music by VICTOR YOUNG

Ev - 'ry star a - bove _____ knows the one I love _____ Sweet Sue, _____ just

you. _____ And the moon up high _____ knows the rea - son why _____ Sweet Sue, _____

_____ it's you. _____ No one else it seems _____ ev - er shares my dream _____ and with -

out you, dear, I don't know what I'd do. _____ In this heart of mine _____ you live

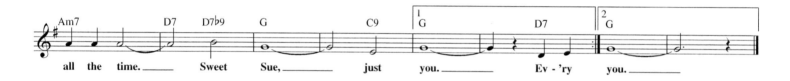

all the time. _____ Sweet Sue, _____ just you. _____ Ev - 'ry you.

TAMMY
from TAMMY AND THE BACHELOR

Words and Music by JAY LIVINGSTON
and RAY EVANS

I hear the cot - ton - woods whis - p'rin' a - bove: Tam - my!
Whip - poor - will, whip - poor - will, you and I know, Tam - my!

Tam - my! Tam - my's {my} {in} love! The ole hoot - ie owl hoot - ie -
Tam - my! Can't let him go! The breeze from the bay - ou keeps

hoo's to the dove: Tam - my! Tam - my! Tam - my's {my} {in}
mur - mur - ing low: Tam - my! Tam - my! You love him

TANGERINE
from the Paramount Picture THE FLEET'S IN

Words by JOHNNY MERCER
Music by VICTOR SCHERTZINGER

TAXI DRIVER
(Theme)
from TAXI DRIVER

By BERNARD HERRMANN

TEACHER'S PET
from TEACHER'S PET

Words and Music by
JOE LUBIN

TEARS IN HEAVEN
featured in the Motion Picture RUSH

Words and Music by ERIC CLAPTON
and WILL JENNINGS

(LET ME BE YOUR) TEDDY BEAR

from LOVING YOU

Words and Music by KAL MANN
and BERNIE LOWE

TENDERLY

from TORCH SONG

Lyric by JACK LAWRENCE
Music by WALTER GROSS

TEQUILA

By CHUCK RIO

(Spoken:)Tequila!

Play 3 times

(Spoken:)Tequila!

THEME FROM "TERMS OF ENDEARMENT"
from the Paramount Picture TERMS OF ENDEARMENT

By MICHAEL GORE

THANK YOU VERY MUCH
from SCROOGE

Words and Music by
LESLIE BRICUSSE

THERE YOU'LL BE
from Touchstone Pictures'/Jerry Bruckheimer Films' PEARL HARBOR

Words and Music by
DIANE WARREN

THANKS FOR THE MEMORY
from the Paramount Picture BIG BROADCAST OF 1938

Words and Music by LEO ROBIN
and RALPH RAINGER

THAT OLD BLACK MAGIC
from the Paramount Picture STAR SPANGLED RHYTHM

Words by JOHNNY MERCER
Music by HAROLD ARLEN

THAT THING YOU DO!
from the Original Motion Picture Soundtrack THAT THING YOU DO!

Words and Music by
ADAM SCHLESINGER

Driving Rock

You,_____ do - in' that thing you do,_____ break-ing my heart in a
I know all the games you play,_____ and I'm gon - na find a
Guitar solo

to a mil - lion piec - es like you al - ways do._____ And
way to let__ you know__ that you'll be mine some day _____ 'cause
Solo ends

you _____ don't mean to be cruel._____ You nev - er e - ven
we _____ could be hap - py, can't you see, _____ if you'd on - ly let me
we _____ could be hap - py, can't you see, _____ if you'd on - ly let me

knew a - bout__ the heart - ache I've been go - ing through._____ Well, I
be the one__ to hold__ you and keep you here with me._____ 'Cause I
be the one__ to hold__ you and keep you here with me._____ 'Cause it

(1., 2.) try and try to for - get you, girl,__ but it's just so hard to do ev - 'ry time you
(3.) hurts me so just to see you go__ a - round with some - one new. And if I know you're

do that thing you do._____ I don't ask a lot,__ girl, but I

know one thing's for sure.__ It's the love I have - n't got,__ girl, and I just can't take it

an - y - more.____ Whoa.__ *D.C. al Coda* **CODA** do - in' that thing ev - 'ry day just

do - in' that thing.__ I can't take you do - in' that thing you do.____

THANK HEAVEN FOR LITTLE GIRLS
from GIGI

Words by ALAN JAY LERNER
Music by FREDERICK LOEWE

THE THIRD MAN THEME
from THE THIRD MAN

Words by WALTER LORD
Based on Music Composed and Arranged by
ANTON KARAS

THAT'S ENTERTAINMENT
from THE BAND WAGON

Words by HOWARD DIETZ
Music by ARTHUR SCHWARTZ

The clown _____ with his pants fall - ing down, ___ or the dance _____ that's a
lights _____ on the la - dy in tights, ___ or the bride _____ with a

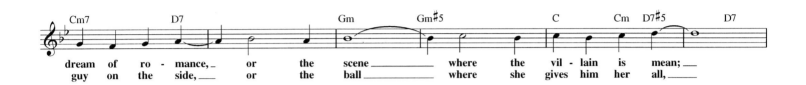

dream of ro - mance, ___ or the scene _____ where the vil - lain is mean; ___
guy on the side, ___ or the ball _____ where she gives him her all, _____

That's en - ter - tain - ment! ___ The
That's en - ter - tain - ment! ___ The

plot can be hot, sim - ply teem - ing with sex, ___ a gay di - vor - cee who is af - ter her "ex."

___ It can be Oe - di - pus Rex _____ where a chap kills his fa - ther, and

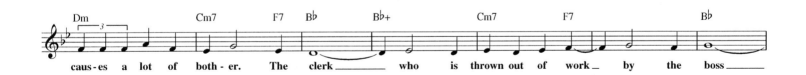

caus - es a lot of both - er. The clerk _____ who is thrown out of work ___ by the boss _____

___ who is thrown for a loss ___ by the skirt _____ who is do - ing him dirt; ___ The

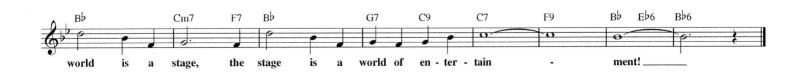

world is a stage, the stage is a world of en - ter - tain - ment! _____

THIS IS HALLOWEEN
from Tim Burton's THE NIGHTMARE BEFORE CHRISTMAS

Music and Lyrics by
DANNY ELFMAN

THAT'S AMORÉ
(That's Love)
from the Paramount Picture THE CADDY
featured in the Motion Picture MOONSTRUCK

Words by JACK BROOKS
Music by HARRY WARREN

THIS IS MY SONG

from Charles Chaplin's A COUNTESS FROM HONG KONG - A Universal Release

Words and Music by
CHARLES CHAPLIN

THREE LITTLE WORDS

from the Motion Picture CHECK AND DOUBLE CHECK

Lyric by BERT KALMAR
Music by HARRY RUBY

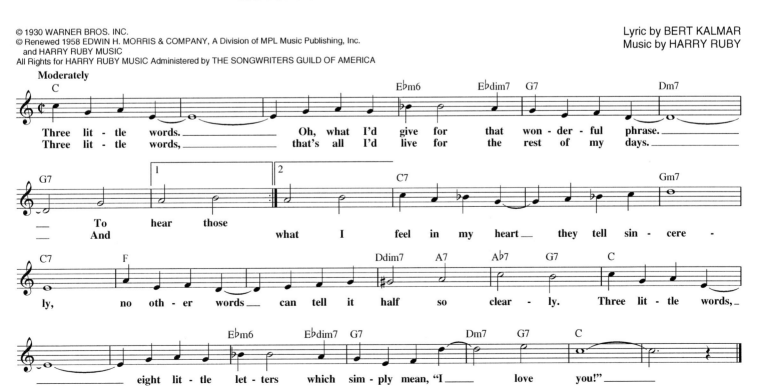

398

THOROUGHLY MODERN MILLIE
from THOROUGHLY MODERN MILLIE

Words by SAMMY CAHN
Music by JAMES VAN HEUSEN

THREE COINS IN THE FOUNTAIN
from THREE COINS IN THE FOUNTAIN

Words by SAMMY CAHN
Music by JULE STYNE

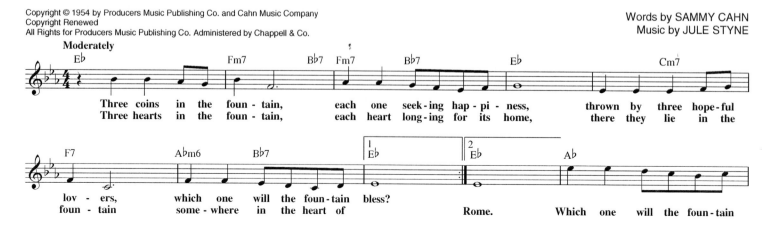

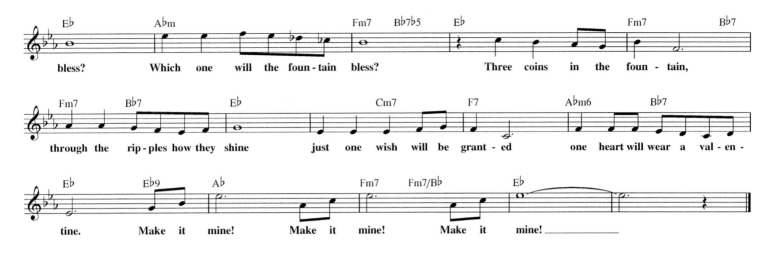

TILL THE END OF TIME
from TILL THE END OF TIME

(Based on Chopin's Polonaise)
Words and Music by BUDDY KAYE
and TED MOSSMAN

A TIME FOR US
(Love Theme)
from the Paramount Picture ROMEO AND JULIET

Words by LARRY KUSIK and EDDIE SNYDER
Music by NINO ROTA

(I'VE HAD) THE TIME OF MY LIFE
from DIRTY DANCING

Words and Music by FRANKE PREVITE,
JOHN DeNICOLA and DONALD MARKOWITZ

401

Additional Lyrics

2. **With my body and soul**
I want you more and more than you'll ever know.
So we'll just let it go,
Don't be afraid to lose control.
Yes, I know what's on your mind
When you say "Stay with me tonight."
Just remember...

THE TIME OF YOUR LIFE
from Walt Disney's A BUG'S LIFE

Words and Music by
RANDY NEWMAN

Moderate 2-Beat

Was a bug, lit - tle bug, hard - ly there. How he felt, what he
Like us all, he start - ed small, then he grew. When the time came, he

dreamed, who would care? With out an - y ev - i - dence
knew what to do. He knew in or - der to suc - ceed

— (his flaws were man - y), he was full of con - fi - dence (some peo - ple have - n't an - y).
— (they'd have to work to - geth - er), turned a rock in - to a seed (and they were changed for - ev - er).

Did - n't have much com - mon sense (it's high - ly o - ver - rat - ed); he just knew that
Then they'd have the strength they'd need (to get through storm - y weath - er). Do or die, you

he'd come through.) It's the time of your life, so live it well. It's the time
got - ta try.

of your life, so live it well. We may on - ly go 'round this

— one time, as far as I can tell. It's the time of your life, it's the time
(He could be wrong a - bout that.)

of your life, it's the time of your life, so live it well.

of your life, so live it well. Is - n't it a bit sur - pris - ing

how our for - tunes ebb and flow? And on - ly to the en - ter - pris - ing does the mag - ic for - tune

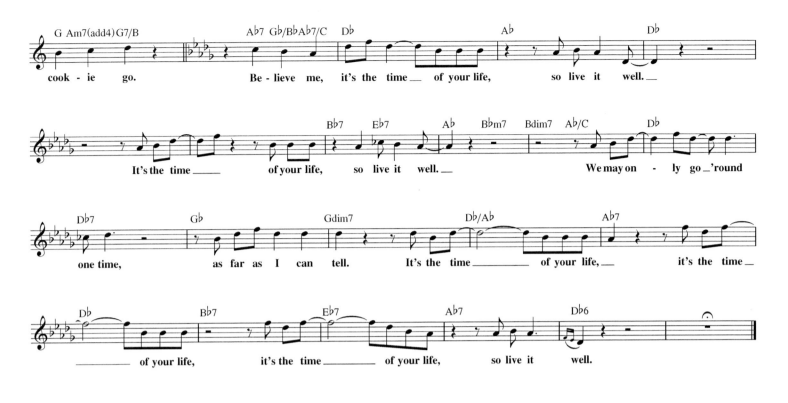

TO EACH HIS OWN
from the Paramount Picture TO EACH HIS OWN
from the Paramount Picture THE CONVERSATION

Words and Music by JAY LIVINGSTON
and RAY EVANS

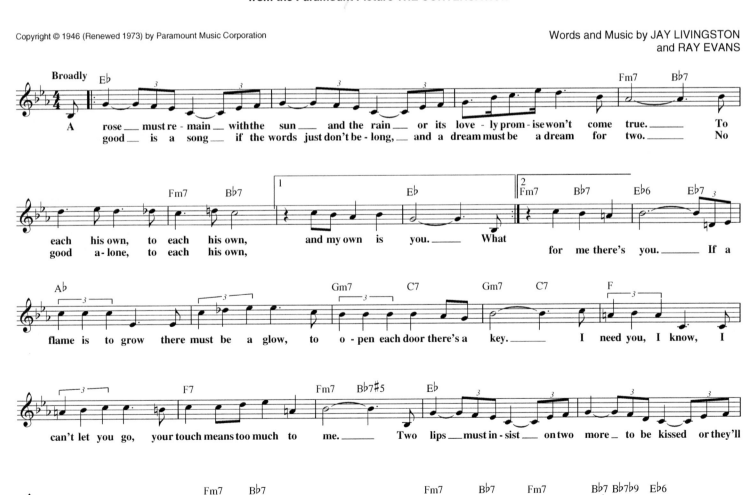

TIME WARP
from THE ROCKY HORROR PICTURE SHOW

Words and Music by
RICHARD O'BRIEN

TO LOVE AGAIN
Theme from THE EDDY DUCHIN STORY

Based on Chopin's E-flat Nocturne
Words by NED WASHINGTON
Music by MORRIS STOLOFF and GEORGE SIDNEY

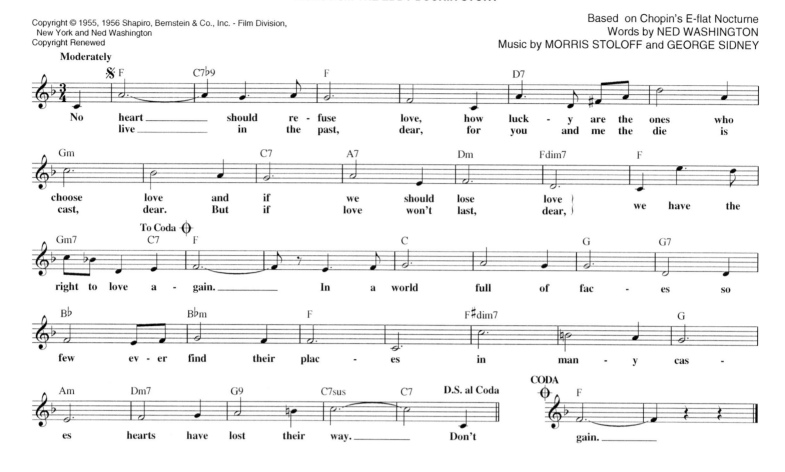

TO SIR, WITH LOVE
from TO SIR, WITH LOVE

Words by DON BLACK
Music by MARC LONDON

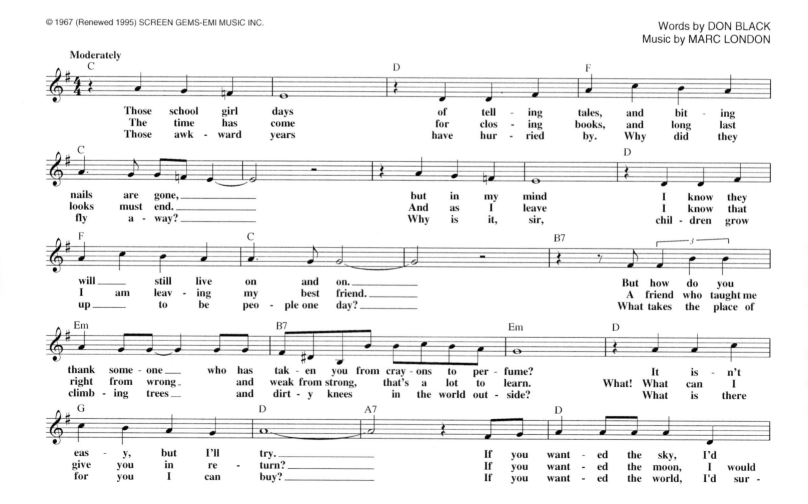

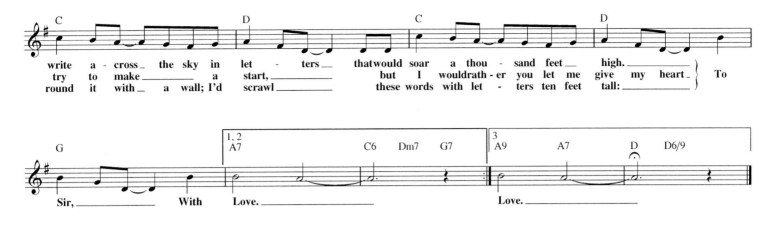

write a-cross_ the sky in let - ters_ thatwould soar a thou - sand feet_ high._
try to make_____ a start,_____ but I wouldrath-er you let me give my heart_ } To
round it with_ a wall; I'd scrawl _____ these words with let - ters ten feet tall: _____

Sir, _____ With Love. _____ Love. _____

TOP GUN ANTHEM
from the Paramount Motion Picture TOP GUN

By HAROLD FALTERMEYER

(Instr. solo ad lib.)

...end solo)

Repeat ad lib. and Fade

TOP HAT, WHITE TIE AND TAILS
from the RKO Radio Motion Picture TOP HAT

Words and Music by
IRVING BERLIN

TOO-RA-LOO-RA-LOO-RAL (THAT'S AN IRISH LULLABY)

from GOING MY WAY

Words and Music by
JAMES R. SHANNON

TRUE GRIT

Theme from the Paramount Picture TRUE GRIT

Words by DON BLACK
Music by ELMER BERNSTEIN

T-U-R-T-L-E POWER!
from TEENAGE MUTANT NINJA TURTLES

By JAMES P. ALPERN
and RICHARD A. USHER, JR.

With a steady beat

N.C.

On the

T - U - R - T - L - E Pow-er. T - U - R - T - L - E pow-er. T - U - R - T - L - E pow-er. Teen-age Mu-tant Nin - ja Tur - tles.

Em   C7

half shell__ they're the he - roes four. In this day and age who could ask for more.__ The
our ace re - port - er was hot on the trail __ de - ter-mined to put__ these crooks in jail.__ The
That was the last straw. Spring in - to ac - tion. Step on "the foot"__ now they're gon - na lose trac - tion.

Asus   C

crime wave is high with mug-gings mys - te - ri - ous All po - lice and de - tec-tives are fu - ri - ous'cause
She spied the bad guys and saw what hap-pened but be - fore she knew it, she fell in the trap __ and got
Now this is for real, so you__ fight for jus - tice. Your shell is hard so you shout, "They can't dust us

Em   C7

they can't find the source of this le - tha - ly e - vil force.
caught. Yeah, she was all a - lone, with no friends and no phone. Now
off like some old __ cof - fee ta - ble." Since you been born __ you been willin' and a - ble to de-

Asus   C

This is se - ri - ous so give me a quar-ter. I was a wit - ness Get me a re - port - er. Call
this was be - yond her worst dreams 'cause she __ was cor - nered by some way-ward teens.__
feat the sneak, pro - tect the weak, fight for rights and your free-dom to speak. __ Now the

Em   C7

A - pril O - Neil in on this case __ eh. You bet - ter hur - ry up. There's no __ time to waste.
Head - ed by Shred-der, they were an - y - thing but good. Mis-guid - ed, un - loved, they called __ 'em "the foot."
vil - lain is chill - in' so you make a stand. Back to the wall, put your sword in your hand.

Asus   C

We need help __ like quick, __ on the dou-ble. Have pit - y on the cit - y, man, __ it's in trou-ble
They could ter - ror - ize and be ___ an - gry youth and they'd mug the peo - ple who __ need - ed proof. Then from the
mem - ber the words of your teach - er, your mas - ter: "E - vil moves fast __ but good __ moves fast - ter than

Em   C7

We need he - roes like __ the Lone Rang - er when Ton - to came pron - to when there was dan - ger.
out of the dark came an awe-some sound. __ Shout-ing "Cow - a - bun - ga" as they hit the ground. From the
light shin-ing for your __ i - lu - min - a - tion." Good ver - sus e - vil equals con - fron - ta - tion. So

Asus   C

Tur - tle

They did - n't say "We'd be there in half an ho - ur," 'cause they dis - played __
field of weeds the he - roes res - cued the flow - er 'cause they pos - sessed __
when you're in trou - ble don't give in and turn sour. Try to re - ly on your

Em   C7   Asus   C

Pow - er.

T - U - R - T - L - E pow-er. T - U - R - T - L - E pow-er. T - U - R - T - L - E pow-er. Teen-age Mu-tant Nin - ja Tur-tles.

TRUE LOVE
from HIGH SOCIETY

Words and Music by
COLE PORTER

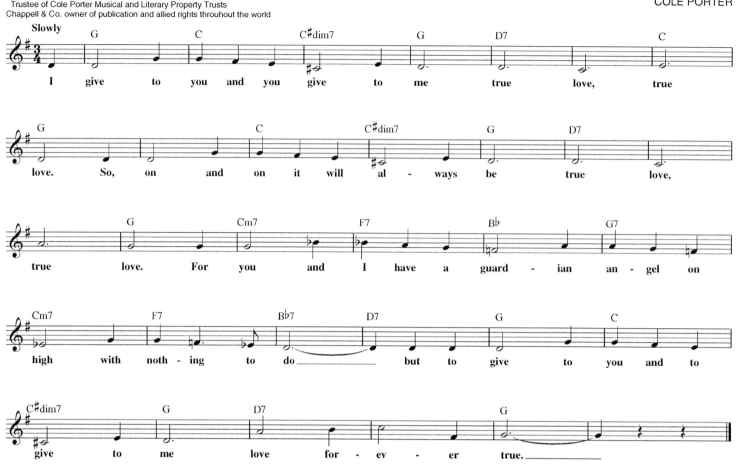

THE UGLY DUCKLING
from the Motion Picture HANS CHRISTIAN ANDERSEN

By FRANK LOESSER

413

UNDER THE SEA
from Walt Disney's THE LITTLE MERMAID

Lyrics by HOWARD ASHMAN
Music by ALAN MENKEN

TWO SLEEPY PEOPLE
from the Paramount Motion Picture THANKS FOR THE MEMORY

Words by FRANK LOESSER
Music by HOAGY CARMICHAEL

UNCHAINED MELODY

Lyric by HY ZARET
Music by ALEX NORTH

UNDERSTANDING

Words and Music by
BOB SEGER

THE UNTOUCHABLES - MAIN TITLE
from the Paramount Motion Picture THE UNTOUCHABLES

Words and Music by
ENNIO MORRICONE

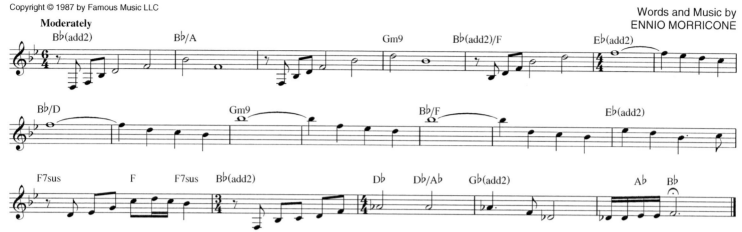

UP WHERE WE BELONG
from the Paramount Picture AN OFFICER AND A GENTLEMAN

Words by WILL JENNINGS
Music by BUFFY SAINTE-MARIE and JACK NITZSCHE

VISIONS OF A SUNSET
from MR. HOLLAND'S OPUS

Words and Music by
SHAWN STOCKMAN

VIVA LAS VEGAS
from VIVA LAS VEGAS

Words and Music by DOC POMUS
and MORT SHUMAN

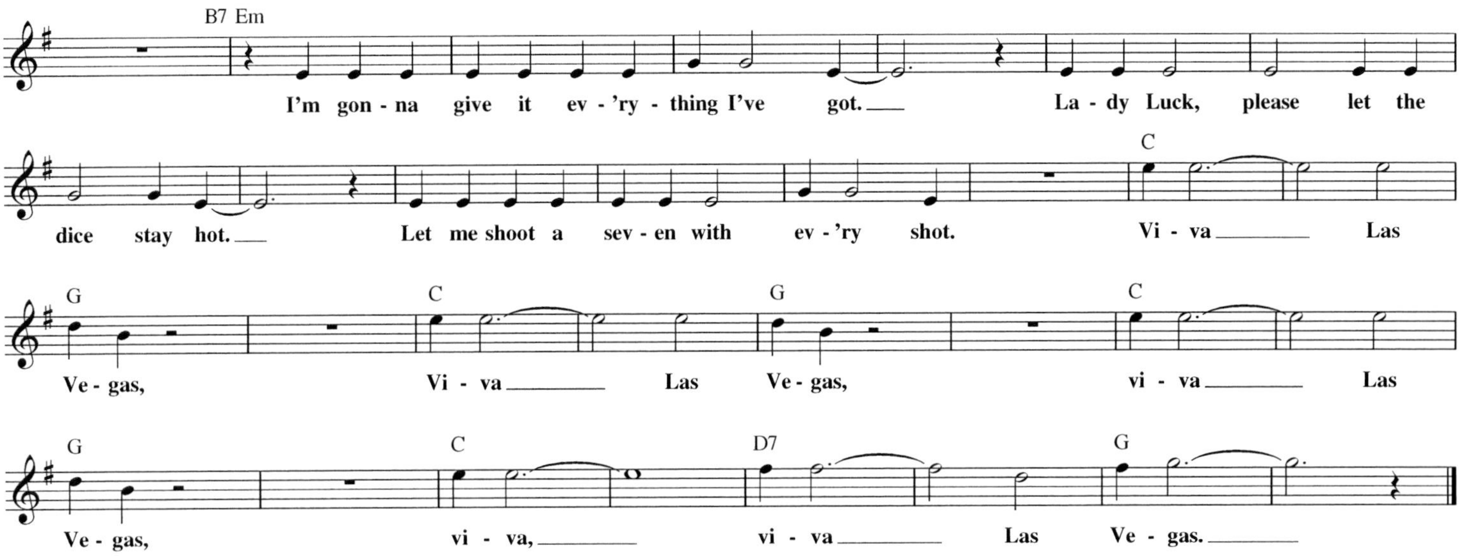

WALK ON THE WILD SIDE
from WALK ON THE WILD SIDE

Lyrics by MACK DAVID
Music by ELMER BERNSTEIN

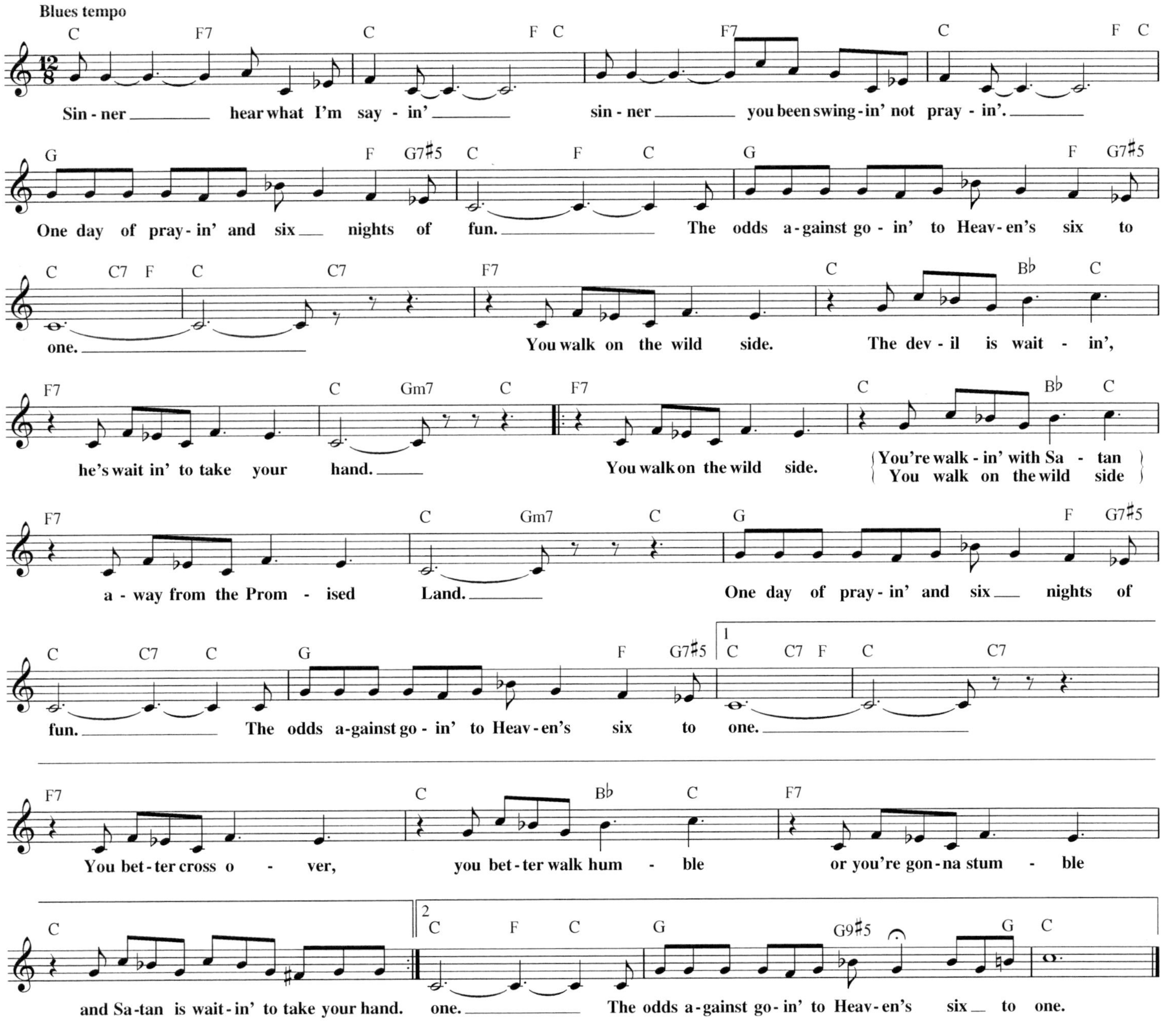

WATCH WHAT HAPPENS
from THE UMBRELLAS OF CHERBOURG

Music by MICHEL LEGRAND
Original French Text by JACQUES DEMY
English Lyrics by NORMAN GIMBEL

THE WAY WE WERE
from the Motion Picture THE WAY WE WERE

Words by ALAN and MARILYN BERGMAN
Music by MARVIN HAMLISCH

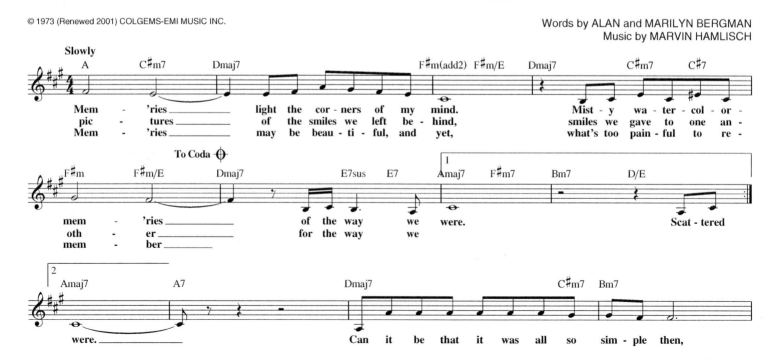

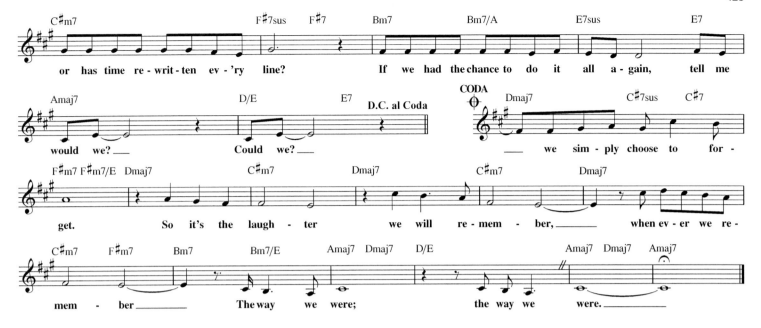

THE WAY YOU LOOK TONIGHT
from SWING TIME
featured in the TriStar Motion Picture MY BEST FRIEND'S WEDDING

Words by DOROTHY FIELDS
Music by JEROME KERN

WE MEET AGAIN
Theme from JERRY MAGUIRE

Words and Music by
NANCY WILSON

Quickly

WEEP YOU NO MORE
from SENSE AND SENSIBILITY

By PATRICK DOYLE

WHAT A WONDERFUL WORLD
Featured in the Motion Picture GOOD MORNING VIETNAM

Words and Music by GEORGE DAVID WEISS
and BOB THIELE

WHAT'S GOOD ABOUT GOODBYE?
from the Motion Picture CASBAH

Lyric by LEO ROBIN
Music by HAROLD ARLEN

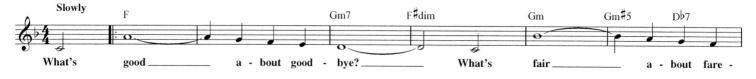

WHAT'S LOVE GOT TO DO WITH IT
featured in WHAT'S LOVE GOT TO DO WITH IT

Words and Music by TERRY BRITTEN
and GRAHAM LYLE

WHEN I FALL IN LOVE
featured in the TriStar Motion Picture SLEEPLESS IN SEATTLE
from ONE MINUTE TO ZERO

Words by EDWARD HEYMAN
Music by VICTOR YOUNG

WHEN I TAKE MY SUGAR TO TEA
from the Paramount Picture MONKEY BUSINESS

Words and Music by SAMMY FAIN,
IRVING KAHAL and PIERRE NORMAN

WHEN SHE LOVED ME
from Walt Disney Pictures' TOY STORY 2 - A Pixar Film

Music and Lyrics by
RANDY NEWMAN

WHEN YOU BELIEVE (From The Prince of Egypt)
from THE PRINCE OF EGYPT

Words and Music by STEPHEN SCHWARTZ
with Additional Music By BABYFACE

WHEN YOU WISH UPON A STAR
from Walt Disney's PINOCCHIO

Words by NED WASHINGTON
Music by LEIGH HARLINE

WHERE DO I BEGIN
(Love Theme)
from the Paramount Picture LOVE STORY

Words by CARL SIGMAN
Music by FRANCIS LAI

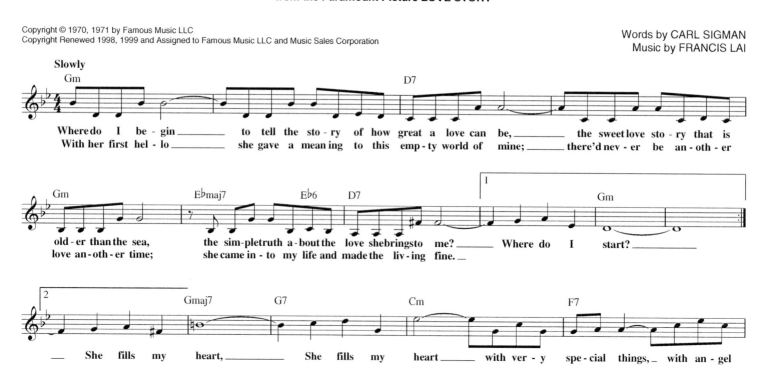

WHERE IS YOUR HEART
(The Song From Moulin Rouge)
from MOULIN ROUGE

Words by WILLIAM ENGVICK
Music by GEORGE AURIC

A WHOLE NEW WORLD
from Walt Disney's ALADDIN

Music by ALAN MENKEN
Lyrics by TIM RICE

WHERE THE BOYS ARE
featured in the Motion Picture WHERE THE BOYS ARE

Words and Music by HOWARD GREENFIELD
and NEIL SEDAKA

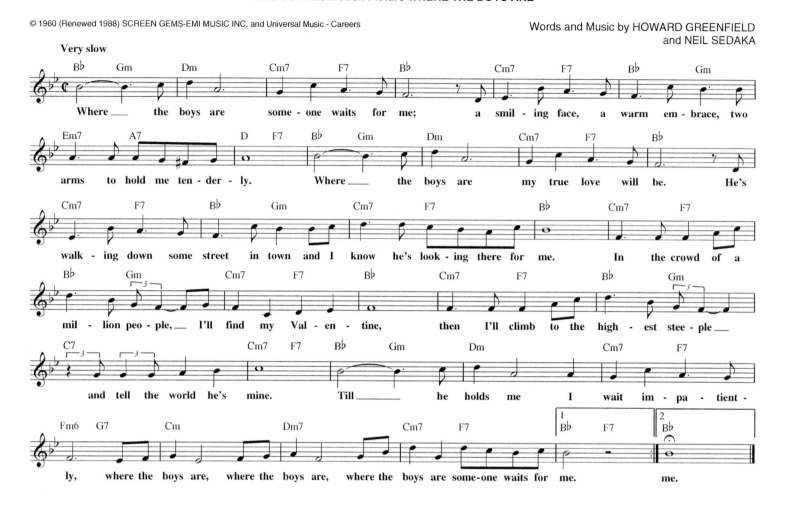

WHO CAN IT BE NOW?
featured in the Motion Picture VALLEY GIRL

Words and Music by
COLIN HAY

THE WINGS
from BROKEBACK MOUNTAIN

By GUSTAVO SANTAOLALLA

A WINK AND A SMILE
featured in the TriStar Motion Picture SLEEPLESS IN SEATTLE

Music by MARC SHAIMAN
Lyrics by RAMSEY McLEAN

WINNIE THE POOH

from Walt Disney's THE MANY ADVENTURES OF WINNIE THE POOH
from Walt Disney's PIGLET'S BIG MOVIE

Words and Music by RICHARD M. SHERMAN
and ROBERT B. SHERMAN

WISH ME A RAINBOW

Theme from the Paramount Picture THIS PROPERTY IS CONDEMNED

Words and Music by JAY LIVINGSTON
and RAY EVANS

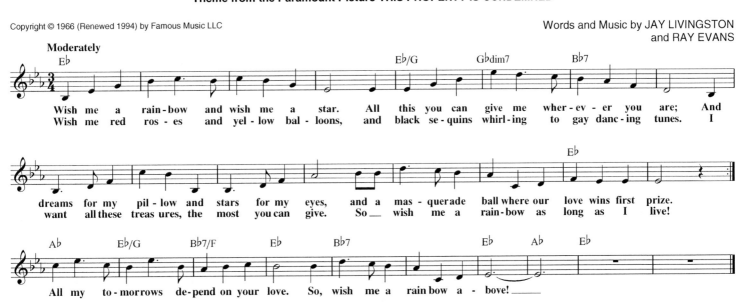

A WOMAN IN LOVE
from the Motion Picture GUYS AND DOLLS

By FRANK LOESSER

WONDERFUL COPENHAGEN
from the Motion Picture HANS CHRISTIAN ANDERSEN

By FRANK LOESSER

YELLOW SUBMARINE

Words and Music by JOHN LENNON
and PAUL McCARTNEY

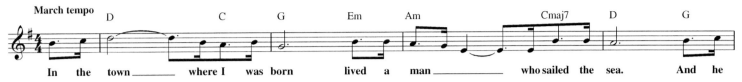

In the town where I was born lived a man who sailed the sea. And he

told us of his life in the land of sub-mar-ines. So we sailed up to the

sun till we found the sea of green. And we lived be-neath the waves in our

yel-low sub-mar-ine. We all live in a yel-low sub-mar-ine, yel-low sub-mar-ine,

yel-low sub-mar-ine. We all live in a yel-low sub-mar-ine, yel-low sub-mar-ine,

yel-low sub-mar-ine. And our friends are all on board, man-y more of them live next
As we live a life of ease, ev-'ry one of us has all we

door. And the band be-gins to play: (Instrumental)
need. Sky of blue and sea of

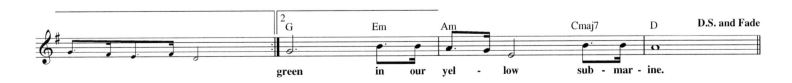

green in our yel-low sub-mar-ine.

YES, YES!

from the Motion Picture PALMY DAYS
from PENNIES FROM HEAVEN

By CON CONRAD
and CLIFF FRIEND

YOU BROUGHT A NEW KIND OF LOVE TO ME

from the Paramount Picture THE BIG POND
from NEW YORK, NEW YORK

Words and Music by SAMMY FAIN,
IRVING KAHAL and PIERRE NORMAN

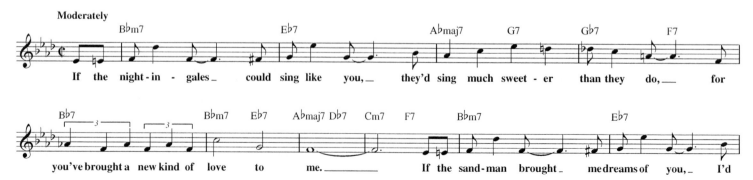

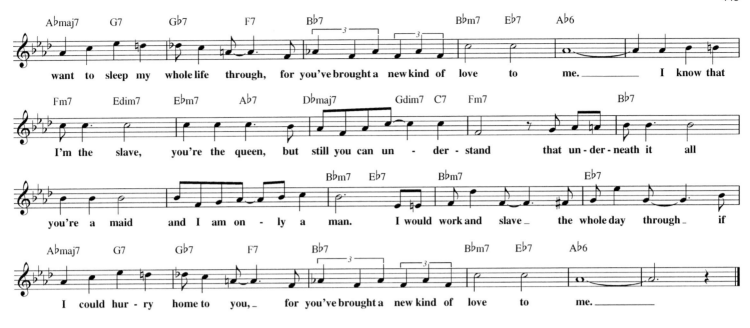

YOU CAN FLY! YOU CAN FLY! YOU CAN FLY!

from Walt Disney's PETER PAN

Words by SAMMY CAHN
Music by SAMMY FAIN

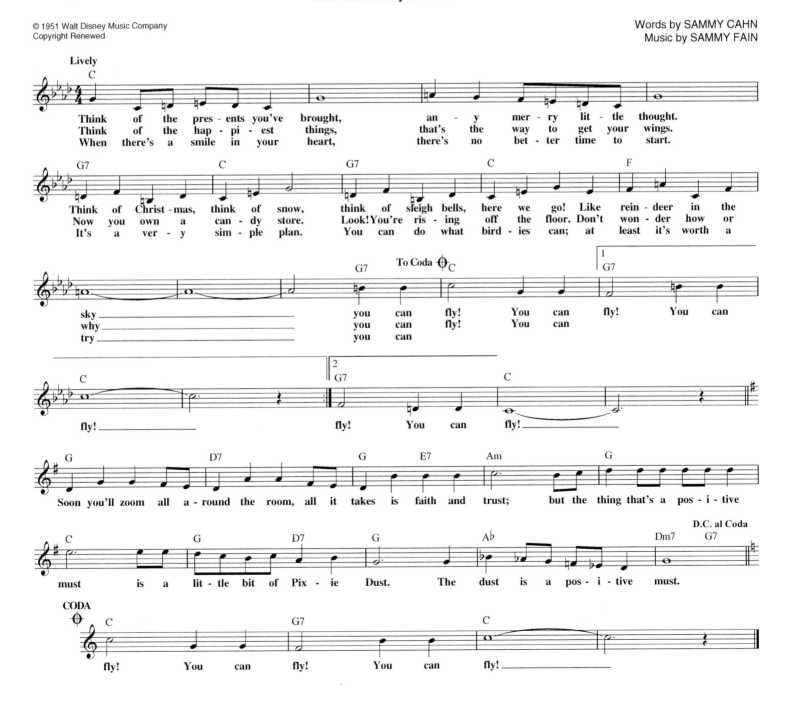

YOU KEEP COMING BACK LIKE A SONG
from BLUE SKIES

Words and Music by
IRVING BERLIN

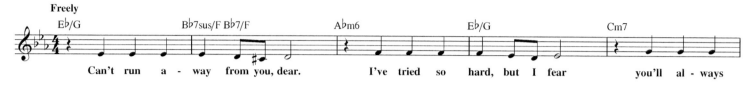

Can't run a - way from you, dear. I've tried so hard, but I fear you'll al - ways

fol - low me near and far. _____ Just when I think that I'm set, just when I've

learned to for - get, I close my eyes, dear, and there you are. _____ You

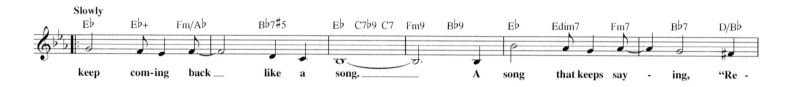

keep com - ing back _____ like a song. _____ A song that keeps say - ing, "Re -

mem - ber." _____ The sweet used-to - be _____ that was once you and me _____

keeps com - ing back _____ like an old mel - o - dy. _____ The per - fume of ros -

- es in May _____ re - turns to my room _____ in De - cem - ber. _____

From out _____ of the past, _____ where for - got - ten things _____ be - long, you

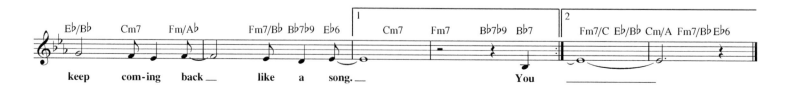

keep com - ing back _____ like a song. _____ You _____

YOU MUST LOVE ME
from the Cinergi Motion Picture EVITA

Words by TIM RICE
Music by ANDREW LLOYD WEBBER

Additional Lyrics

2. *(Instrumental 8 bars)*
Why are you at my side?
How can I be any use to you now?
Give me a chance and I'll let you see how
Nothing has changed.
Deep in my heart I'm concealing
Things that I'm longing to say,
Scared to confess what I'm feeling
Frightened you'll slip away,
You must love me.

YOU SHOULD BE DANCING
from SATURDAY NIGHT FEVER

Words and Music by BARRY GIBB,
ROBIN GIBB and MAURICE GIBB

Moderately, with a beat

My (D.S.) ba - by moves at mid - night, ___ goes right on till the dawn; ___ my
juic - y and she's trou - ble, ___ she gets it to me good; ___ my

wom - an takes me high - er, my wom - an keeps _ me warm. ___ What you
wom - an gives me pow - er, goes right down to ___ my blood. ___

do - in' on your back, aah, ___ what you do - in' on your back, aah? ___ You should be

Danc - in, ___ yeah, ___ danc - in', ___ yeah. ___ She's ___ What you

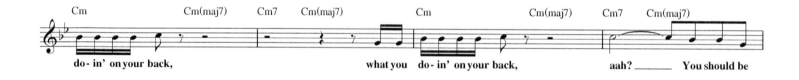

do - in' on your back, what you do - in' on your back, aah? ___ You should be

danc - in', ___ yeah, ___ danc - in', ___ yeah. ___ (Instrumental)

My

YOU'D BE SO NICE TO COME HOME TO
from SOMETHING TO SHOUT ABOUT

Words and Music by
COLE PORTER

YOU'RE NEARER
from TOO MANY GIRLS

Words by LORENZ HART
Music by RICHARD RODGERS

YOU'LL BE IN MY HEART
(Pop Version)
from Walt Disney Pictures' TARZAN™

Words and Music by
PHIL COLLINS

YOU WERE LOVED

from the Touchstone Motion Picture THE PREACHER'S WIFE

Words and Music by
DIANE WARREN

In a slow 2

We all wan-na make a place in this world. We all want our voic-es to be heard.
dia-monds in your hands, have all the rich-es in the land,

Ev-'ry-one wants a chance to be some-one.
but with-out love, you don't real-ly have a thing, no, no.

We all have dreams we need to dream, sweet-er than an-y star you can reach.
Will some-bod-y care that you're a-live? Will some-bod-y trust you with their life?

'Cause when you reach and find you
That's when you'll know that you have all

found some one, you'll hold their world's most price-less thing, the great-est gift
you need. You hold the world's most price-less gift, the fi-nest treas-

that life can bring. 'Cause when you look back and know you were loved
-ure that there is, 'cause you can look back and know

You were loved by some-one, touched by some-one, held by some-one, meant

some-thing to some-one, loved some-bod-y, touched some-bod-y's heart a-long the way.

1.
You can look back and say, mm,

you were loved. Yes, you were, You can have

YOU'VE GOT A FRIEND IN ME
from Walt Disney's TOY STORY
from Walt Disney Pictures' TOY STORY 2 - A Pixar Film

Music and Lyrics by
RANDY NEWMAN

YOUNG AT HEART
from YOUNG AT HEART

Words by CAROLYN LEIGH
Music by JOHNNY RICHARDS

Slowly

Fair - y tales ___ can come true, ___ it can hap - pen to you ___ if you're young at heart. _____
know ___ that it's worth ___ ev - 'ry treas - ure on earth ___ to be young at heart. _____

___ For it's hard, ___ you will find, ___ to be nar - row of mind ___ if you're
For as rich ___ as you are, ___ it's much bet - ter by far ___ to be

young at heart. _____ You can go ___ to ex - tremes ___ with im -
young at heart. _____ And if you ___ should sur - vive ___ to a

pos - si - ble schemes, ___ you can laugh ___ when your dreams ___ fall a - part at the seams ___ and
hun - dred and five ___ look at all ___ you'll de - rive ___ out of

life gets more ex - cit - ing with each pass - ing day, ___ and love is ei - ther in your heart or

on the way. ___ Don't you be - ing a - live, ___ and here is the best part, ___

you have a head start ___ if you are a - mong the ver - y young at heart. ___

ZIP-A-DEE-DOO-DAH
from Walt Disney's SONG OF THE SOUTH

Words by RAY GILBERT
Music by ALLIE WRUBEL

Brightly

Zip - a - dee - doo - dah, Zip - a - dee - ay, ___ my, oh my, ___ what a

won - der - ful day! ___ Plen - ty of sun - shine, head - in' my way, ___ Zip - a - dee - doo -

- dah, Zip - a - dee - ay! ___ Mis - ter Blue - bird on my shoul - der, ___ it's the

truth it's "act - ch'll," ev - 'ry - thing is "sat - is - fact - ch'll." Zip - a - dee - doo - dah,

Zip - a - dee - ay! ___ Won - der - ful feel - ing, won - der - ful day. ___

ZORRO'S THEME
from the TriStar Motion Picture THE MASK OF ZORRO

Written and Composed by
JAMES HORNER

Guitar Chords

C	C	Cm	C+	Csus	C5	Cdim	Csus2	C(add9)	C6	Cmaj7	C7
C♯/D♭	C♯	C♯m	C♯+	C♯sus	C♯5	C♯dim	C♯sus2	C♯(add9)	C♯6	C♯maj7	C♯7
D	D	Dm	D+	Dsus	D5	Ddim	Dsus2	D(add9)	D6	Dmaj7	D7
E♭/D♯	E♭	E♭m	E♭+	E♭sus	E♭5	E♭dim	E♭sus2	E♭(add9)	E♭6	E♭maj7	E♭7
E	E	Em	E+	Esus	E5	Edim	Esus2	E(add9)	E6	Emaj7	E7
F	F	Fm	F+	Fsus	F5	Fdim	Fsus2	F(add9)	F6	Fmaj7	F7
F♯/G♭	F♯	F♯m	F♯+	F♯sus	F♯5	F♯dim	F♯sus2	F♯(add9)	F♯6	F♯maj7	F♯7
G	G	Gm	G+	Gsus	G5	Gdim	Gsus2	G(add9)	G6	Gmaj7	G7
A♭/G♯	A♭	A♭m	A♭+	A♭sus	A♭5	A♭dim	A♭sus2	A♭(add9)	A♭6	A♭maj7	A♭7
A	A	Am	A+	Asus	A5	Adim	Asus2	A(add9)	A6	Amaj7	A7
B♭/A♯	B♭	B♭m	B♭+	B♭sus	B♭5	B♭dim	B♭sus2	B♭(add9)	B♭6	B♭maj7	B♭7
B	B	Bm	B+	Bsus	B5	Bdim	Bsus2	B(add9)	B6	Bmaj7	B7

459

Root											
C	C7sus	C7#5	C7b5	C7b9	C7#9	C7#11	Cmaj7#11	C6/9	Cmaj9	C9	C9sus
C#/Db	C#7sus	C#7#5	C#7b5	C#7b9	C#7#9	C#7#11	C#maj7#11	C#6/9	C#maj9	C#9	C#9sus
D	D7sus	D7#5	D7b5	D7b9	D7#9	D7#11	Dmaj7#11	D6/9	Dmaj9	D9	D9sus
Eb/D#	Eb7sus	Eb7#5	Eb7b5	Eb7b9	Eb7#9	Eb7#11	Ebmaj7#11	Eb6/9	Ebmaj9	Eb9	Eb9sus
E	E7sus	E7#5	E7b5	E7b9	E7#9	E7#11	Emaj7#11	E6/9	Emaj9	E9	E9sus
F	F7sus	F7#5	F7b5	F7b9	F7#9	F7#11	Fmaj7#11	F6/9	Fmaj9	F9	F9sus
F#/Gb	F#7sus	F#7#5	F#7b5	F#7b9	F#7#9	F#7#11	F#maj7#11	F#6/9	F#maj9	F#9	F#9sus
G	G7sus	G7#5	G7b5	G7b9	G7#9	G7#11	Gmaj7#11	G6/9	Gmaj9	G9	G9sus
Ab/G#	Ab7sus	Ab7#5	Ab7b5	Ab7b9	Ab7#9	Ab7#11	Abmaj7#11	Ab6/9	Abmaj9	Ab9	Ab9sus
A	A7sus	A7#5	A7b5	A7b9	A7#9	A7#11	Amaj7#11	A6/9	Amaj9	A9	A9sus
Bb/A#	Bb7sus	Bb7#5	Bb7b5	Bb7b9	Bb7#9	Bb7#11	Bbmaj7#11	Bb6/9	Bbmaj9	Bb9	Bb9sus
B	B7sus	B7#5	B7b5	B7b9	B7#9	B7#11	Bmaj7#11	B6/9	Bmaj9	B9	B9sus

C	C9#5	Cmaj9#11	C9#11	C9b13	C11	C13	C13b9	C7#5(b9)	C7#5(#9)	C7b9(b13)	C7#9(b13)
C#/Db	C#9#5	C#maj9#11	C#9#11	C#9b13	C#11	C#13	C#13b9	C#7#5(b9)	C#7#5(#9)	C#7b9(b13)	C#7#9(b13)
D	D9#5	Dmaj9#11	D9#11	D9b13	D11	D13	D13b9	D7#5(b9)	D7#5(#9)	D7b9(b13)	D7#9(b13)
Eb/D#	Eb9#5	Ebmaj9#11	Eb9#11	Eb9b13	Eb11	Eb13	Eb13b9	Eb7#5(b9)	Eb7#5(#9)	Eb7b9(b13)	Eb7#9(b13)
E	E9#5	Emaj9#11	E9#11	E9b13	E11	E13	E13b9	E7#5(b9)	E7#5(#9)	E7b9(b13)	E7#9(b13)
F	F9#5	Fmaj9#11	F9#11	F9b13	F11	F13	F13b9	F7#5(b9)	F7#5(#9)	F7b9(b13)	F7#9(b13)
F#/Gb	F#9#5	F#maj9#11	F#9#11	F#9b13	F#11	F#13	F#13b9	F#7#5(b9)	F#7#5(#9)	F#7b9(b13)	F#7#9(b13)
G	G9#5	Gmaj9#11	G9#11	G9b13	G11	G13	G13b9	G7#5(b9)	G7#5(#9)	G7b9(b13)	G7#9(b13)
Ab/G#	Ab9#5	Abmaj9#11	Ab9#11	Ab9b13	Ab11	Ab13	Ab13b9	Ab7#5(b9)	Ab7#5(#9)	Ab7b9(b13)	Ab7#9(b13)
A	A9#5	Amaj9#11	A9#11	A9b13	A11	A13	A13b9	A7#5(b9)	A7#5(#9)	A7b9(b13)	A7#9(b13)
Bb/A#	Bb9#5	Bbmaj9#11	Bb9#11	Bb9b13	Bb11	Bb13	Bb13b9	Bb7#5(b9)	Bb7#5(#9)	Bb7b9(b13)	Bb7#9(b13)
B	B9#5	Bmaj9#11	B9#11	B9b13	B11	B13	B13b9	B7#5(b9)	B7#5(#9)	B7b9(b13)	B7#9(b13)

	Cm#5	Cm6	Cm7	Cm(maj7)	Cm7b5	Cdim7	Cm(add9)	Cm9	Cm6/9	Cm(maj9)	Cm11
C											

	C#m#5	C#m6	C#m7	C#m(maj7)	C#m7b5	C#dim7	C#m(add9)	C#m9	C#m6/9	C#m(maj9)	C#m11
C#/Db											

	Dm#5	Dm6	Dm7	Dm(maj7)	Dm7b5	Ddim7	Dm(add9)	Dm9	Dm6/9	Dm(maj9)	Dm11
D											

	Ebm#5	Ebm6	Ebm7	Ebm(maj7)	Ebm7b5	Ebdim7	Ebm(add9)	Ebm9	Ebm6/9	Ebm(maj9)	Ebm11
Eb/D#											

	Em#5	Em6	Em7	Em(maj7)	Em7b5	Edim7	Em(add9)	Em9	Em6/9	Em(maj9)	Em11
E											

	Fm#5	Fm6	Fm7	Fm(maj7)	Fm7b5	Fdim7	Fm(add9)	Fm9	Fm6/9	Fm(maj9)	Fm11
F											

	F#m#5	F#m6	F#m7	F#m(maj7)	F#m7b5	F#dim7	F#m(add9)	F#m9	F#m6/9	F#m(maj9)	F#m11
F#/Gb											

	Gm#5	Gm6	Gm7	Gm(maj7)	Gm7b5	Gdim7	Gm(add9)	Gm9	Gm6/9	Gm(maj9)	Gm11
G											

	Abm#5	Abm6	Abm6	Abm(maj7)	Abm7b5	Abdim7	Ab(add9)	Abm9	Abm6/9	Abm(maj9)	Abm11
Ab/G#											

	Am#5	Am6	Am7	Am(maj7)	Am7b5	Adim7	Am(add9)	Am9	Am6/9	Am(maj9)	Am11
A											

	Bbm#5	Bbm6	Bbm7	Bbm(maj)7	Bbm7b5	Bbdim7	Bbm(add9)	Bbm9	Bbm6/9	Bbm(maj9)	Bbm11
Bb/A#											

	Bm#5	Bm6	Bm7	Bm(maj7)	Bm7b5	Bdim7	Bm(add9)	Bm9	Bm6/9	Bm(maj9)	Bm11
B